THE LIBRARY OF EDUCATIONAL THOUGHT

Edited by C. H. Dobinson

ARISTOTLE

ARISTOTLE

His thought and its relevance today

CYRIL WINN and MAURICE JACKS

METHUEN & CO LTD
11 NEW FETTER LANE · LONDON EC4

First published 1967 by Methuen & Co Ltd

Printed in Great Britain by
Richard Clay (The Chaucer Press) Ltd, Bungay, Suffolk

Distributed in the U.S.A.
by Barnes & Noble, Inc.

Contents

Illustrations

Preface

Aristotle was born into a group of people who, thanks partly to a well-developed system of slavery, had established a way of life which involved the strenuous use of the intellectual, aesthetic, physical, and moral capacities of human beings. Thanks to automation, the world just ahead can, and must, establish a similar way of life. So the thoughts of Aristotle upon education – thoughts of one of the greatest minds of all time – have a startling and challenging relevance to us today.

The two men who have here garnered for us some of Aristotle's most interesting views on education are both of them men who, in their own intellectual development were exposed to the mind of Aristotle and, no doubt, unconsciously advantaged by this. But also they are men who have themselves made important developments in educational thought and practice. The late Maurice L. Jacks, who died when only the framework and one or two chapters had been completed, was one of the first of the group of very young headmasters who brought important new developments to the Public Schools after the First World War – he was only twenty-nine when he was appointed headmaster of Mill Hill School. Here, among other pioneer achievements, he developed a broad conception of physical education along lines which Plato and Aristotle had adumbrated, replacing the former ex-Army Sergeant-Major tradition of physical training by an integrated series of bodily activities both using, and acting upon, the mind. Years later he transformed the Oxford University Department of Training into the Oxford University Department of Education, and by his own brilliant and unanswerable logic, after some years of effort, brought about the founding of the Oxford University Institute of Education. His books, including *Modern Education*, *Total Education*, and *The Education of Good Men*, and the publications resulting from a series of annual conferences with Industry on the Education of the Young Worker, had meanwhile spread new thoughts and set on foot new experiments which later blossomed into established practices of today, for example, the provision of liberal education as a concomitant and outgrowth of all forms of technical education.

Cyril Winn, who took over the manuscript after the death of M. L. Jacks, was a former solo chorister of St Paul's Cathedral, Scholar of Exeter College, Oxford, Classical Master at a Grammar School and, later, H. M. Chief Inspector of Music. But, before his musical gifts, his personality and his vision had added much to the musical life of the schools of England and Wales, he had achieved brilliant success as principal of one of the ill-fated Day Continuation Schools – schools which, had they not been abandoned by faint-hearted local and central government when attacked by selfish and shortsighted business and industrial interests, would have probably made England and Wales the land fit for heroes that Lloyd George had set out to build. In Cyril Winn's Day Continuation School, at the southern foot of Tower Bridge, reluctant van-boys found themselves, in a few weeks, transformed into self-ruling citizens, running choirs, and the whole gamut of sports clubs.

How fitted, therefore, is Cyril Winn to bring to fruition this book on Aristotle – one of the earliest believers in State control of education – and one of the authorities of his time on music in education.

Indeed, in this little book Cyril Winn has made available to educators what is probably the most readable account, to be found in print anywhere today, of Aristotle's views on music in education, so for decades teachers of music round the world will be in debt to him. But not they alone – for all who read this book will be grateful to him for seeing that the manuscript which the late Maurice Jacks had embarked upon at the time of his passing was fully developed, expanded and rounded off as a work both of scholarship and of challenge to new thought.

C. H. DOBINSON

I · Of Aristotle and his Philosophy

Although Aristotle was not, until the present century, regarded as so important a figure as Plato in the matter of educational theory, he was undeniably the more practical of the two. One is aptly reminded of Raphael's famous painting in Rome, styled 'The School of Athens', in which Plato is depicted as pointing heavenwards, and Aristotle as pointing earthwards; and that, of course, metaphorically is the main difference between them. The latter was a realist – he has been called 'a hard intellectualist' – whereas the former was the idealist, the dreamer, the lover of myth.

But Aristotle, like Plato his teacher, for whom he professed a profound admiration, was a master of many sciences, and, indeed, there was scarcely a single subject on which he did not dilate; and he dilated with consummate insight. His most original contribution to scientific study, however, was his work in biology, which demanded the kind of classification and tabulation of objects, both animate and inanimate, in which he was engrossed. It is no wonder, therefore, that he has always been known as the 'Father of Biology'.

Thus it is to this modern age, which is not especially distinguished for planning and looking ahead, that the views of Aristotle on Education should prove interesting; not only as introducing many fresh aspects of the subject, but also because in many ways they are strikingly modern. Moreover, he was evidently expressing the ideas and opinions of the most intellectual and forward-looking men of his day; though some of these ideas were not put into actual practice until after his death.

He asserts that the theory and practice of education must, without question, be built upon a solid foundation of a philosophy of life, especially in the fields of ethics and politics. Such a building he constructs for us; and it is very significant that his books important for this purpose are the *Nicomachean Ethics* (named after his father, Nichomachus) and the *Politics*. Much of what he writes about education is not especially related to any one time or place. Though, of course, Aristotle had the background of Athenian education in his mind, yet his thought is of universal significance. It not only throws light on many of today's problems but it is of the utmost value in recalling us to first principles. So we need to know the philosophical background to it. Who, then, was Aristotle and what did he think?

Aristotle was born in 385 B.C. at Stagirus, a small city on the North East coast of Greece, that is, on the fringe of the Greek world. He was therefore not an Athenian but an Ionian, and from his home town he was thus able to study the excellences and defects of the more famous city-states of Greece. His father, Nichomachus, was a member of the medical profession and court physician to Amyntas I, King of Macedon. At the age of seventeen he was sent to Athens for higher education in philosophy and science, and entered the famous Platonic Academy, where he was brought into close relationship with the profoundest thinker Greece had yet produced.

After Plato's death in 347 B.C. he left Athens and lived for three years with a former fellow-student, Hermeas by name, who had become 'Tyrant' in Mysia, and whose daughter he married. This experience must have given him inside information of the workings of a 'Tyranny' (Chapter 2), about which he had subsequently much to say. When later, however, the country was overrun by the Persians, Aristotle fled to the neighbouring island of Lesbos. But he had not to wait long for a change of fortune, for in 342 B.C. Philip, King of Macedon, invited him to act as tutor to his son, Alexander, then a lad of thirteen. Plutarch in his *Lives* assures us that the son showed a like respect for his tutor, as did his father, asserting that 'to the one he owed life, and to the other the good life'. In 336 B.C., when Alexander succeeded his father on the throne of Macedon, Aristotle returned to Athens. Arrived home, he broke away completely from the old Academy and became the head of a distinguished School of Philosophy in the Lyceum. Here, where his lectures were given, was a Gymnasium, or public wrestling-place, with covered walks, in the eastern suburbs of Athens, named after the neighbouring temple of Apollo Lyceias (the wolf-like), and surrounded by a colonnade. One of the original features of his 'method' was the fact that he walked up and down as he lectured. It may be remembered by some that the late Sir Henry Hadow, when lecturing on Aristotle's *Ethics* at Worcester College, Oxford, used to perambulate the hall for a whole hour, radiating wit and wisdom the while – which *might* be regarded as an indirect influence of Aristotle's teaching on a modern educator! At any rate, the Lyceum became the centre of the Peripatetic School of Philosophy (*peripatein* – to walk about), as distinct from the Academy, where Plato's students gathered. Both these outstanding schools of thought, though diverging in many respects from each other, fundamentally had more in common, for were they not both indirect offshoots of the teaching of the architectonic philosopher Socrates himself?

It was during these years, no doubt, that frequent discussions on ethics and politics took place, as a result of which these two works – the latter unfinished – with which we are mainly concerned, took shape. At the Lyceum Aristotle presided for fourteen years; in fact, until the death of his royal pupil.

There is little doubt that Alexander's regard for Greek philosophy, and his admiration for Greek culture, was due largely to Aristotle's teaching and influence, though it is unlikely that the latter, or indeed any loyal subject of a city-state, would have approved of the conqueror's policy, when he had subdued the whole of Greece, to merge Greeks and 'barbarians' as equals in his empire. This policy meant also the collapse of so much that was essential to, and characteristic of, the political life of Greece. And so it came about, after Alexander's death, that a revolt broke out, sponsored by the Athenians, in the hope of regaining independence. Although it was short-lived, all those who sympathized with Macedon, of whom Aristotle, with his former connexions, was considered to be one, became suspect. Public opinion, in fact, was so strong against him that he was driven into exile on a charge of impiety, and thus probably escaped the fate of Socrates. His place of exile was none other than the Macedonian citadel of Colchis, the mother city of his native Stagirus, where he died in the following year.

The method to be adopted in this chapter of extracting the value of Aristotle's thought on education is that of summarizing the ideas contained in relevant passages, and subsequently, in later chapters, working over these in relation to modern problems and ideas. The summaries are broken up into sections (I A, I B, etc.) and their relation to modern problems and ideas are figured 2 A, 2 B, etc., for purposes of reference. It has been thought better to summarize Aristotle's conclusions for the most part, rather than to quote his words in full for reasons of space. Moreover, in the course of his writings he discusses many conflicting views, only to discard them after further reasoning; and, as is well known, there is a good deal of repetition. On occasion, however, when the context requires it, the quotation is indicated by inverted commas, and is reproduced by kind permission of the Loeb Classical Library.

We begin with a summary of Aristotle's philosophy, compiled by Maurice Jacks, in relation to ethics and politics, drawn mainly from passages in the two books bearing those titles.

1 A

The ultimate end for man is the Good, and the highest good is happiness. But happiness is not a disposition (not a mere state or condition as Plato asserts), but the activity of the soul's faculties in conformity with virtue, that is to say, living the 'good life'. It is a lifelong process, and is the aim of all; it should not be regarded as a means, but rather as an end desirable in itself (*Eth.* I, 7 and 8).

The highest happiness is an activity in conformity with the highest value, call it the best part of us, or theoretical knowledge (*Eth.* X, 7). Therefore the life of the intellect will be the happiest, the life of moral virtue being happy only in a secondary degree. Perfect happiness is some form of contemplative activity, and distinguishes man from the animals. If happiness consists in well-doing, it follows that the life of action is best, alike for every State as a whole, and for each individual in his own conduct, for the happiness of the former is the same as that of the latter. But the life of action *need* not be a life which involves relations with others. For thoughts with no special action beyond themselves, and speculations followed solely for their own sake, are far more deserving of the name of 'active' than more conventional activities. Happiness, incidentally, implies an adequate provision of external goods (*Eth.* VI, 1).

1 B

Virtue is a disposition of the mind consisting essentially in the observance of the 'Mean'. If this is true, and if a truly happy life is a life of goodness, it follows that the best and happiest life is one which consists in a Mean attainable by every individual (*Eth.* II, 6).

I C

The soul consists of two parts; one possesses a rational principle intrinsically and as part of its nature; the other has not, but is capable of obeying such a principle. The part which has the rational principle is the higher part, and may in turn be divided into two parts of its own – speculative or scientific, of which the virtue is wisdom, and practical, or deliberative, of which the virtue is prudence. Ideally the soul rules the body as a master, and the mind rules the appetites as a monarch (*Eth.* I, 13).

> Virtue being of two kinds, intellectual and moral, intellectual virtue is, for the most part, both produced and increased by instruction, and therefore requires experience and time; whereas moral or ethical virtue (*ēthos*) is the product of habit (*ēthos*), and has indeed derived its name from that word. It is clear, therefore, that none of the moral virtues is engendered in us by nature, for no natural property can be altered by habit (*Eth.* II, 1).

Therefore nature gives us the capacity to receive them, and this capacity is brought to maturity by habit. For example, we become temperate by abstaining from pleasures when we have become temperate. An index of our habits of acting is afforded by the pleasure or pain that accompanies our actions; for pleasure causes us to do base actions, and pain causes us to abstain from doing noble actions. Hence the importance, as Plato points out, of having been definitely trained from childhood 'to like and dislike the proper things; this is what good education means' (*Eth.* II, 1 and 3; X, 1).

I D

The City–State (*polis*) grows for the sake of life, but exists primarily for the sake of the *good* life; for man is by nature an animal destined to live in a *Polis.* A natural impulse is therefore one reason for living a social life; a common interest is another, but men also come together merely for the sake of life (*Eth.* II, 3, and *Pol.* II, 5).

The *Polis* is an aggregate of many members, and education is *the* one means of converting it into a community and giving it unity. It should achieve goodness by means of an educational system which calls to its aid social custom, intellectual culture, and legislation. The aim of the *Polis* is not mere life but rather a good quality of life. So if a constitution is to survive, all the elements in the *Polis* must combine to will its maintenance. The best means of ensuring this, therefore, is the education of the citizens in the spirit of their constitution. There is no profit in the best of laws if the citizens have not been attuned, by the force of habit and the influence of teaching, to the right constitutional temper – whether of democracy or of oligarchy, or of any other type (*Pol.* III, 4; 5 sec. 14; 7 sec. 6; V, 7 sec. 20).

The education of a citizen in the spirit of the constitution consists in his doing the actions by which the particular form of government may be enabled to survive. We must not regard a citizen as belonging merely to himself but as belonging to the *Polis*. His excellence must be an excellence relative to the constitution, and a *Polis* is good in virtue of the goodness of the citizens who share in its government. All should share alike in a system of government under which they rule and are ruled by turns. The laws, however, should be sovereign on every issue, and the magistrates and citizens should decide only on matters of detail. The sort of people whom a legislator can easily guide into the way of goodness are those gifted with a natural endowment which combines intelligence with spirit. Thus individuals become good by three means; natural endowment, the habits which they form, and the rational principle within them. It is more important to equalize men's desires (by keeping them under control) than their properties; and this can be done only by an adequate moral training, such as the laws determine. There must certainly be equality in education, but not one and the same for all (*Pol.* V, 9).

I E

Experience supports the testimony of theory, that it is the duty of the lawgiver rather to study how he may frame his legislation both with regard to warfare and in other departments for the object of leisure and of peace. Most military states remain safe while at war, but perish when they have won their empire; in peace-time they lose their keen temper, like iron. The lawgiver is to blame, because he did not educate them to employ lesiure. And since it appears that men have the same end, both collectively and individually, and since the same distinctive aim must necessarily belong both to the best man and to the best government, it is clear that the virtues relating to leisure are essential. To occupy leisure nobly is the first principle of all things. For although both business and leisure are necessary, yet leisure is more desirable, and more fully an end, than business; so we must inquire what is the proper occupation of leisure. Assuredly it could not be employed in play, since it would follow that play is our end in life. But this is impossible, and sports should rather be employed in our times of business (for a man who is at work needs rest, and rest is the object of play, while business is accompanied by toil and exertion). So it follows that in introducing sports we must watch the right opportunity for their employment, since we are applying them to serve as medicine: for the activity of play is a relaxation of the soul, and serves as recreation because of its pleasantness. But leisure seems itself to contain pleasure and happiness and felicity of life. And this is not possessed by the busy but by the leisured; for the busy man busies himself for the sake of some end as not being in his possession, but happiness is an end achieved, which all men think is accompanied by pleasure, and not by pain. But all men do not go on to define pleasure in the same way, but according to their own characters and their various natures . . . So that it is clear that some subjects must be learnt and acquired merely with a view to the pleasure in their pursuit, and that these studies and these branches of learning are ends in themselves, while the forms of learning related to business are studied as necessary and as means to other things. Hence our predecessors included music in education not as a necessity . . . but as a pastime in leisure . . . But the virtues useful for leisure and its employment are not only those that operate during leisure, but also those that operate in business; for many of the necessaries must needs be forthcoming to give us opportunity for leisure. Therefore it is proper for the state to be temporate, brave, and enduring; since, as the proverb says 'there is no leisure for slaves', but people unable to face danger bravely are the slaves of their assailants. Therefore courage and fortitude are needed for business, love of wisdom for leisure, temperance and justice for both seasons, and more especially when men are at peace, and have leisure; for war compels men to be just and temperate, whereas the enjoyment of prosperity and peaceful leisure tend to make them insolent. Therefore much justice and much temperance are needed by those who are deemed very prosperous, the more they are at leisure and have an abundance of such blessings. It is clear, therefore, why a state that is to be happy and righteous must share in these virtues; for if it is disgraceful to be unable to use our good things, it is still more disgraceful to be unable to use them in time of leisure (*Pol.* VII, 13).

I F

Since property is a part of a household, and the art of acquiring property a part of household management (for without the necessaries even life, as well as the good life, is impossible), and since, just as for the definite arts it would be necessary for the proper tools to be forthcoming if their work is to be accomplished, so also the manager of a household must have his tools. And of tools some are lifeless and others living; so an article of property also is a tool for the purpose of life, and property generally is a collection of tools, and a slave is a live article of property, and every assistant is, as it were, a tool that serves for several tools; for if every tool could perform its own work when ordered or by sensing what to do in advance – if thus shuttles wove and quills played harps of themselves – master-craftsmen would have no need of assistance, and masters no need of slaves (*Pol.* I, 5).

It is clear then that household management takes more interest in the human members of the household than in its inanimate property, and in the excellence of these than in that of its property, which we style riches, and more in that of its free members than in that of slaves. First of all then as to slaves, the difficulty might be raised, does a slave possess any other excellence besides his merits as a tool and a servant, more valuable than these, for instance, temperance, courage, justice, and any of the other moral virtues, or has he no excellence beside his bodily service? For either way there is difficulty; if slaves do possess moral virtue, wherein will they differ from freemen? Or if they do not, this is strange, as they are human beings and participate in reason. We have laid it down that the slave is serviceable for the mere necessaries of life, so that clearly he needs only a small amount of virtue, in fact just enough to prevent him failing in his tasks owing to intemperance and cowardice. But the question might be raised, supposing that what has just been said is true, will artisans also need to have virtue? for they frequently fall short in their tasks owing to intemperance, or is their case entirely different? For the slave is a partner in his master's life, but the artisan is more remote, and only so much of virtue falls to his share as of slavery [i.e. his excellencies as an artisan are the qualities of a subordinate, his virtues as a human being, apart from his trade, are not considered], for the mechanic artisan is under a sort of limited slavery. It is manifest, therefore, that the master ought to be the cause to the slave of the virtue proper to a slave, but not as possessing the art of mastership which teaches a slave his tasks. Hence those persons are mistaken who deprive the slave of reasoning, and tell us to use command only: for admonition is more properly employed with slaves than with children (*Pol.* I, 5).

1 G

Now we consider that much is well said on these matters [the ethical value of certain types of music] by some of the musicians of the present day and by some of those engaged in philosophy who happen to be experienced in musical education, and we will abandon the precise discussion as to each of these matters for any who wish to seek it from those teachers, while, for the present, let us lay down general principles, merely stating the outline of the subjects.

And since we accept the classification of melodies made by some philosophers as ethical melodies, melodies of action, and passionate melodies [i.e. representative of character, of action, and emotion] . . . we say that music ought to be employed both for education and for purgation. [In the *Poetics* VI tragedy is said to purge the emotions of pity and fear by giving them an outlet] and thirdly for amusement, serving to relax our tension and to give rest from it. It is clear that we should employ all the melodies, yet not employ them all in the same way, but use the most ethical ones for education, and the active and passionate kinds for listening to when others are performing (*Pol.* VIII, 7).

2 A

It is significant that this opening paragraph should exist as a philosophical basis for the theory and practice of education. Aristotle does not embark on this until he has considered:

(i) the end for man, both as an individual and a citizen, for which he will have to be educated; this is the teleological (*telos* = end) view of education, which will be referred to later under this same section (A);
(ii) the psychology of man;
(iii) what constitutes a full life for him, and the conditions under which it will have to be lived.

This approach to education may well be contrasted with our largely haphazard, hand-to-mouth procedures, dictated too often by expediency and political considerations rather than by philosophic principles.

We may not approve of Aristotle's conclusions, of course, but we cannot ignore the fact that they are there for all to 'read, mark, learn, and inwardly digest'. We may perhaps accept happiness, in his interpretation of the word, as the proper end for man, but we must also view it in the light of the Christian tradition, when it becomes greatly enriched, as in the 'Sermon on the Mount'. 'Happy are you who are poor: the Kingdom of God is yours.' 'Happy are you who weep now: you shall laugh.' 'Happy are you who now go hungry: your hunger shall be satisfied' – and the like. We must then consider how far it is right that one of the principal aims of education should be to turn out people capable of attaining a well-considered ideal of *happiness* and how it can be done.

The idea that the 'highest happiness is some form of contemplation' while 'the life of moral virtue is happy only in a secondary degree' is one which is unfamiliar to the modern world [1]. It is bound up with Aristotle's teleological view of education, which seeks to discover in children what they are striving to become by observing the kind of things which at any given moment they are interested in doing; for a full account of that activity may give some clue as to the purpose that they are individually eager to realize. Thus the highest good for any living organism is to be discovered in the full flowering of its nature; and that involves the realization of all its endowments, of which, Aristotle adds, the most distinctive for man is reason, for it is this which distinguishes him from plants and animals. So it is that the end of man must be sought in the life guided by reason.

But reason is of two kinds; practical and speculative or theoretical. The former is concerned with social and political activity, that is, with conduct, because man is a 'social and political animal'; above all, it is concerned with the observance of the Mean. But the latter form of reason is devoted to speculative activity, that is, the activity of the pure intellect or spirit, which is pursued for its own sake, and moves in the region of truths which are immutable and universal. And since this activity is, as we have seen, the most distinctive and the highest activity in man, therefore the highest kind of good life – and accordingly of happiness – is to be found in its exercise.

It must not be supposed, however, that the virtue of practical reason is confined to the ordinary man; on the contrary, it is an essential requisite of the good life of the leisured intellectual as well. But while the ordinary man regards the virtue of practical reason as an end in itself, the sage sees it only as a means. We may summarize this in the words of the late Professor C. E. M. Joad: 'Thus the good life is in the last resort the life of the mind, in the widest sense of that word, whether it is devoted to creation in art, to the quest of knowledge in scientific research, or to that contemplation of the essential nature of things which some have called philosophy, and others mysticism' [2]. This exaltation of reason as the mainspring of orderly thought and action is, of course, a characteristic of ancient Greek thought, but can it be said to be holding a like position in the disordered world of today? Or are the fields of nuclear physics and of cosmology glorious exceptions and worthy continuations of Greek thought at its highest?

2 B

What does Aristotle signify by the statement that 'Virtue is to be found in adherence to a Mean'? His answer would be that the nature of good acts is that of a mean or balance. Right actions, therefore, cannot be judged by themselves, but only in relation to the extremes on either side of them. For example, 'the observance of the mean in fear and confidence is courage. He that exceeds in confidence is rash; he that is deficient in confidence is cowardly'.

The doctrine is based on an analogy between the mind and the body. It was the medical view in those days that bodily health consisted in a balance between extremes of heat and cold, dry and moist, and the like. To disturb this balance by taking too much or too little food was to impair health; and so with the minds and characters of men.

Support for this doctrine of the mean as the road to right behaviour is by no means confined to Aristotle. We ourselves are only too familiar with such expressions as 'Enough is as good as a feast' and 'Wisdom consists in knowing where to stop'. It is characteristically expressed by Lord Chesterfield in one of his letters: 'The sure characteristic of a sound mind is to find in everything those certain bounds beyond which it is not right to traverse. These boundaries are marked out by a very fine line . . . In manners, this line is good breeding: beyond it, is troublesome ceremony: short of it, is unbecoming negligence and inattention. In morals, it divides ostentatious puritanism from criminal relaxation: in religion, superstition from impiety; and, in short, every virtue from its kindred vice or weakness.' We learn also that the doctrine holds considerable sway among the peoples of China, having been originally advocated by Confucius in his ethical teachings. This view of life as being determined by an observance of the mean might imply that it is apt to become stereotyped. But Aristotle, stressing the importance of habit, recommends that our estimate of the mean should become so habitual that, when faced with a moral problem, we should act automatically, without having to consider the matter deeply [2].

'On the other hand, would the doctrine be adequate to satisfy the moral conscience of a man where self-sacrifice, unselfishness, and courage was demanded of him? It suggests a too-calculating frame of mind, measuring, as it were, the quantity of good which he intends to do in the world. The doctrine has often been regarded as more suitable for middle age than for youth. There is no doubt, however, that this middle-of-the-road course was the one set for the majority of our people also, in the last century, at any rate' [2].

It is not easy to understand how the Greeks arrived at this particular moral precept, for it is clear that the principle of the Mean was the guide which accompanied them throughout their lives, whether they all observed it or not. 'Was it the result of brooding over the miserable fate of those, on the one hand, who had grown helpless and useless to the State in a life of unbridled excesses, and had come to a tragic end? On the other hand, there were the cowards and traitors who had, by their actions, endangered the safety of the State, and so had earned the disapproval of the whole community. But the principle does imply the ability to see life whole, and on all its sides' [3].

2 C

Aristotle's psychology and conception of the whole man, physical, irrational (not guided by reason) and rational – and all subject to education – is greatly over-simplified when contrasted with the complexities of its modern counterpart; but it is workable and useful. It is the last sentence of 1 C, however, which conveys the kernel of Aristotle's views on education, and once and for all justifies the English attempt *in school* to give not merely learning but training in group loyalty, in sportsmanship, in responsibility and in self-government; that children should be trained by habit from childhood 'to like and dislike the right things'. It is pleasing to reflect that Aristotle acknowledges his debt to Plato in so fundamental a pronouncement.

2 D

In what sense does Aristotle describe man as a 'political animal', and how far can we accept his inference as to man's function and duties as a citizen, and the part to be played by education in preparing him for these? The modern version of this 'political animal' and modern conceptions of education in citizenship will be discussed in the next chapters. Meanwhile he seems to believe here in learning by doing: but is he right? Do children learn to be citizens by *being* citizens? If so, what are the implications for education?

2 E

Aristotle's division of life into occupation, leisure, and recreation is very relevant to the modern social, economic, and industrial situation. There is, of course, considerable overlapping, and the content of each section is much richer and more diversified than was the case in Aristotle's day. But the distinction still stands, and, translated into modern terms, deserves much closer attention than it normally receives. This is particularly so with the distinction between leisure and recreation, not only as regards the best ways of catering for the former, but also as to the education necessary for this.

2 F

This conception of a slave economy follows necessarily from two considerations. First, if the pursuit of knowledge is the highest type of the good life – and this was clearly beyond the capacity of the ordinary man to achieve – there must be some who are called upon to provide the necessities of life in order that the few – the leisured sages – may enjoy their 'high thinking', untrammelled by thought of menial work. Secondly, as the *Polis* exists in order to promote the good life, and this is only for the few to achieve, they must be provided for by 'the many'. In Greece some of 'the many' happened to be slaves – and their proportion of the population was by no means small – but it must be conceded that in that country slaves were comparatively well treated; in fact, their general conditions of life compared very favourably with those experienced by the average maid-of-all-work in the ordinary household of the Victorian age. Today, of course, they are largely replaced by machines, and Aristotle, with remarkable insight, realized this possibility, pointing out that mechanical inventions, which he describes as 'inanimate tools', may take the place of 'living tools', which would render slaves unnecessary (*Pol.* I, 2).

In any case, the high level attained by Athenian civilization, for example, was only possible because the 'chores' were done by 'animated tools' (slaves) who were regarded mainly as machines. Thanks to the monotonous labours of large masses of the population a comparatively small number of Greeks had been able to live the highly cultivated life they did [4].

Is this assumption and acceptance of a slave economy a necessary condition for the civilized life of any community? The evidence of history is strong against it, and we have only to glance at the disordered state of the world today, in Africa, Asia, and the United States, to understand what destruction and ruin slavery, directly or indirectly, has brought upon the world.

The position today is that the machine, especially the automated machine, is the slave, and so the situation is becoming strikingly parallel to that in Aristotle's day. For the existence of some form of slave economy, human or machine, was a basic assumption in Aristotle's educational programme.

2 G

Here we have yet another example of Aristotle's determination to base his theory and practice of education on a basic philosophy of life. In the matter of music this is so involved as to need a chapter to itself.

All these issues will be discussed in detail in subsequent chapters.

2 · The Aims of Education

I A

To recapitulate: if happiness, as activity according to goodness, is accepted as the end for men, and if the highest goodness is to be found in the life of the intellect, two of the aims of education, goodness and intellectual development, are implicitly determined.

Happiness belongs to those who have cultivated their character and mind to the utmost, and kept the acquisition of external goods within moderate limits, more than to those who have acquired more of these than they can possibly use, and are lacking in the goods of the soul (*Eth.* I, *passim*).

> A man's happiness is equal to the amount of his goodness and his wisdom, and goodness is of two kinds, intellectual and moral. Intellectual virtue is, for the most part, produced and increased by instruction, and therefore requires experience and time; whereas moral virtue is the product of habit. The capacity to develop moral virtue is given us by nature and is brought to maturity by habit (*Eth* II, 1).

The importance of having been definitely trained from childhood 'to like and dislike the proper things' is what good education means (*Eth.* II. 3). The pupil must thus be trained to become a good citizen of the *Polis* (city-state), whatever its constitution, and must be educated in the spirit of that constitution. It will be remembered also that under 1 D Aristotle refers to the *Polis* as an aggregate of many members, and stresses that education is the chief means of turning it into a community and giving it unity; for the purpose of the *Polis* is not mere life; it is a good quality of life: thus, the best means of ensuring the stability of their constitution.

1 B

Tyrannies preserve themselves, *inter alia*, by forbidding education (in other words by a defensive attitude against everything likely to produce mutual confidence and high spirits). The legislator must labour to ensure that his citizens become good men, and must know what institutions will produce this result, as well as what is the end to which a good life is directed (*Pol.* IV, 2, 6 and 8; *Eth.* VIII, 10).

1 C

The citizens must be able to lead a life of action and war; but they must be even more able to lead a life of leisure and peace. It is true that they must be able to do necessary or useful works; but they must be even more able to do good acts. These are the general aims which ought to be followed in the education of childhood, *and of the stages of adolescence which still require education*. The qualities of courage and endurance are required for the activities of occupation; while wisdom is required for those of leisure; temperance and justice are required at both times and under both heads – though especially in times of leisure and peace (*Pol.* VII, 14).

I D

Some states in the training of youth seek to create an athletic habit of body, but do so at serious cost both to the figure and to the growth of the body. This is an error; for it turns the young into savages, under the mistaken notion that this is the best way of fostering the virtue of courage. It is, therefore, a mistake to direct the training of youth exclusively or mainly to this one virtue.

Indeed, there are several other important ingredients in the training for moral virtue, and among them is music.

> Our predecessors included music in education not as a necessity, (for there is nothing necessary about it) nor as useful in the way in which reading and writing are useful for business and for household management . . . nor yet again as we pursue gymnastics, for the sake of health and strength. . . . It remains, therefore, that it is useful as a pastime in leisure, which is evidently the purpose for which people actually introduce it; for they rank it as a form of pastime for free men.
>
> Nevertheless we must examine whether it is not the case that the nature of music is more honourable than corresponds with the employment of it mentioned [i.e. as a pastime] but to see if its influence reaches also in a manner to the character and to the soul; and it would clearly be the case if we are affected in our characters in a certain manner by it. But it is clear that we *are* affected in a certain manner both by many kinds of music, and not least by the melodies of Olympus [a Phrygian composer of the 7th century B.C.] for these make our souls enthusiastic, and enthusiasm is an affection of the character of the soul. And moreover everybody when listening to imitations [i.e. music dramatically expressing various states of emotion] is thrown into a corresponding state of feeling, even apart from the rhythms and tunes themselves. From these considerations therefore it is plain that music has the power of producing a certain effect on the moral character of the soul, and, if it has the power to do this, it is clear that the young must be directed to music, and must be educated in it.
>
> Our first enquiry is whether music ought not or ought to be included in education, and what is its efficacy among the three uses of it that have been discussed – for education, or amusement, or intellectual enjoyment. It is reasonable to reckon it under all of these heads, and it appears to participate in them all (*Pol.* VIII, 2–5).

2 A

If happiness as an activity according to intellectual and moral goodness, and within the grasp of all, is accepted as the proper end for man, it follows that the main aim of education must be to turn out those capable of attaining this.

It would appear that three main elements are required for this:

(i) teaching what is meant by happiness as an activity and its connexion with goodness;
(ii) intellectual development;
(iii) character-training.

(i) As has been previously noted (*Eth.* I), Aristotle's conception of happiness is a very limited one, particularly in view of the high place he accords to the life of intellectual contemplation, compared with the Christian conception of it.

His conception, therefore, must be enriched, as already suggested, by the Christian view of happiness. Moreover, the working out of a happiness according to age, ability, and aptitude is a problem awaiting considerable research, at any rate, in the United Kingdom. This would therefore amount to a relative, and not an absolute, happiness. It might well be achieved by a self-expressive sharing in the activities of a 'good school', a spiritual community, to which it must obviously be the general aim to attain. In such a school, in one or more of the many activities open to him, every pupil will find the happiness suited to his ability and aptitude. Intellectual activity will, of course, figure among these, but it will not necessarily be the 'best'. The happiness of our State, therefore, will consist in each individual child or adult discovering his true nature and gifts, finding his place in the community, and making his maximum contribution to it. This should guarantee his happiness – as opposed to his pleasure – and the happiness of the whole, which would seem to be our modern reinterpretation of Aristotle's somewhat limited outlook on the subject.

(ii) The development of intellectual goodness means primarily good teaching, both of the intellectually capable as well as of the rest. But until schools have large library *spaces* in which pupils can follow-up quietly and individually the inspiring lessons they have had, often from the radio and from television, closed circuit or public, there will continue to be too much teaching and too little learning. The aim throughout schooling should be the fostering of mental alertness, of curiosity, of interest, and with these also of a critical and questioning outlook – the first aim in the teaching of any and every subject. But do the university departments of education and the colleges of education prepare their students for transmitting this critical approach of the individual mind?

(iii) Character training is an essential part of Aristotle's or any other's plan for education. We pay lip-service to it, but have we ever thought it out? What right have we to mould a character, and what is the mould? Aristotle says that the ideal character is one which will best promote the happiness of the State, but can we accept this? Where does *individual* happiness come in to the picture? The answer seems to be that there are three elements in this training:

(*a*) a conception of goodness wide enough to include being *good at something*, for there is no goodness in a vacuum; and the door is clearly open to vocational training;

(*b*) a training in the moral virtues, generally accepted by society; above all, the inculcation of habits of 'liking and disliking the proper things' (*Eth*. II, 3);

(*c*) the recognition of the character-potentialities of each individual, though they may be those of a rebel. It is only by this means that individual happiness may be attained. This point of view, be it noted, Aristotle does not recognize.

2 B

(i) In the matter of education for citizenship, we are set to discover on what grounds it is justified as one of the aims of modern education. Primarily it involves the transformation of the crowd into the community, and this the right kind of education is best fitted to achieve.

(ii) That the function of education to educate its pupils in the spirit of the constitution, whatever that may be, even if it is a bad one, is a thought which is quite unacceptable. For a 'tyranny' or dictatorship is often the enemy of education, or its friend only if it is at the mercy of the political dictates of the ruling power.

We have already seen many examples of this in Hitler's Germany, as we are still seeing it today in Franco's Spain, where the universities stand opposed to the dictates of the ruling power. But could the indoctrination of dictatorship be displayed more blatantly than in a true picture of four hundred small children in a school in Genoa (August 1931) marching round the hall for a considerable time, and chanting 'Viva Mussolini' as they paraded? Needless to say, there was a gigantic portrait of the *Duce* hanging over the headmistress' desk for all to see. Also we have other parallels in pre-war Japan and today even in Africa.

Our view is that we should teach our pupils *about* democracy, and the democratic way of life, but not *for* it.

(iii) This is achieved partly by the pupil in his school 'doing the actions by which a democracy will be enabled to survive', and that means everything in the life and organization of a school. In this great undertaking all schools are necessarily involved, but certain types, like the Comprehensive and the Independent Boarding (Public) schools, have special opportunities and responsibilities for cultivating the democratic way of life, the former by reason of their size, and the latter because their pupils are 'settled' there for the whole term. Whether the mere size of the Comprehensive school is an argument against it or not, the fact remains that it has wider scope for experiment than most of turning the crowd into a community. The Public school, on the other hand, is, by its very nature, already a 'community' in virtue of the fact that its pupils lead a communal life, working, feeding, and sleeping under the same roof, as it were. This means greater opportunity, but, at the same time, no less responsibility in this matter.

In general, and strictly speaking, there can be no question of *inducing* this community spirit, because it is there already – an unsuspected energy awaiting liberation in *most* human beings. Man is *naturally co-operative* – a born co-operator – a fact often overlooked, though needing to be greatly stressed whenever education, either of *children* or of adults, is in question. Whether we study the constitution of his mind or his body, we find at every point that the activity his structure demands and is fitted for is not isolated, but co-operative. The man is made to co-operate with the woman, and vice-versa, the parent with the child, the teacher with the pupil, and so on – why else is he endowed with the faculty of speech? He works best, on the whole, when he is working with others; he plays best when he plays against another. Indeed, he should be thought of as playing *with* him, since, without an antagonist, there would be no game at all. Man needs an 'antagonist' both for work and for play – and his 'antagonist' is often his best friend!

(iv) That 'The future citizen must learn to rule and be ruled, and to share in a way of life in which this will happen' is a maxim as necessary today as it was in Aristotle's, and involves a consideration of deterrents and punishments for those who object to being ruled. Summary punishments, that is, those inflicted by 'dispensing with needless details and formalities' and done 'with dispatch' might well be ruled out in our schools. G. K. Chesterton in his whimsical book *The Club of Queer Trades* tells an imaginary story of a judge who, on giving sentence on a man who had attempted a crime of passion, said, 'I sentence you to three years' imprisonment, under the firm, solemn, and God-given conviction that what you require is three months at the seaside!' This was indeed a very exaggerated case of assessing a judgment, but it was, at least, original. In days gone by most industrial schools could boast of a numerous and very vigorous brass band – an excellent plan for giving recalcitrant lads an opportunity for 'blowing off steam' down a brass tube of some sort. Here the severest punishment for any member of the band was to be deprived of his instrument for a time. In any case, ought not such vital factors as heredity and, above all, environment, to be taken into account when the nature of the punishment is being considered? This is a consideration which, surely, demands deep and careful thought, especially with children. In some of the more adventurous schools, both of the past and of today, there have been formed a small council or committee of prefects to assess the degree of the offender's indiscipline, and to suggest a fair and just penalty. There may be dangers in this plan, of course, partly through their inexperience of life, but, at least, they probably know more about the hidden life – 'a skeleton in the cupboard' maybe – of their school-fellows than do their masters, however sympathetic *they* may be. For all this a tremendous responsibility – and 'tremendous' in its very literal sense – is thrust upon the teacher, for his final decision as to the nature of the punishment may have lasting results for good or evil.

(v) If 'the good citizen is the good man', this throws a wholly new light on education. True it is that in recent years 'religious instruction' has been made compulsory in all schools, but we may well doubt whether it has had the desired effect of producing 'good children'. There are many thinking men and women, Humanists and Agnostics among them, who would like to see the Act repealed. But what should be put in its place? Should attendance be made voluntary? If so, only the potentially 'better' children – possibly those who like singing hymns – would attend. But if all continue to attend, as they do now, might not some of the seed, though sown on stony ground, some day bring forth fruit, even if not to perfection?

2 C

Education for leisure is indeed a matter of urgency today, and of increasing urgency in the future, as human labour is becoming more and more displaced by scientific machinery. We now euphemistically refer to this as 'redundancy', but 'unemployment' is the stark word for it. Enforced leisure is truly as dangerous as enforced labour. The four-day week and the four-hour day is slowly but inevitably descending upon us, and the burning question is, what is to be done with the many idle hours remaining? Aristotle's 'slave population' has vastly increased, and is increasing every day, and we are faced with the same educational problem which faced him – but we have failed to solve it. Indeed, we have been far more successful in education for clerical occupations as well as for memorizing facts to suit various examiners than for leisure. In the latter, despite a good deal of lip-service to it, and some half-hearted attempts at it, the evidence of present-day conditions proves hat we have failed. Children have not been taught to be *active* in their leisure occupation; but good citizenship depends far more on the *quality of what is done in leisure time* – as in occupation, of course – than on a training in the spirit of the Constitution or anything else. Aristotle's threefold analysis is valuable and pertinent, and particularly his distinction between leisure and the other two. It needs, however, certain emendations and additions:

(i) Labour and leisure cannot be kept in separate compartments, because they have constant inter-action, especially where the Arts are concerned. In particular they cannot be educated for separately, and to talk of 'education for leisure' may be dangerous; except, of course, in the case of the employee whose work is solely repetitive. Our aim, therefore, must be to educate the whole man, so that he will be good at both.

(ii) There is constant overlapping between the three – occupation, leisure-activity, and recreation. One man's occupation will be another man's leisure-activity, and a third man's recreation. Music, for example, may be the occupation of one – the professional, the leisure activity of another – the amateur, and the recreation of yet a third – the listener.

(iii) Aristotle's virtues of courage, wisdom, and the like, will be needed, as he asserts, and must *form* the educational aim, but that is not the whole story. We need to add:

(iv) self-activity (which he describes simply as 'activity') in skill and creation, for which man is fitted biologically but commonly unprepared educationally, *and* the satisfaction of man's natural 'skill-hunger';

(v) high standards of performance, whether at work or play, or in leisure, and the recognition that anything from cooking a meal to governing a State may be a work of art if well done. This applies also to speculative thinking, which in Aristotle's view is the happiest form of activity, as well as to the more conventional forms of activity. Ideally, leisure activities should be self-made, and not dependent upon the labour of others. This should be a delight to the leisured and a benefit to the others. The aims of education for leisure should therefore be:

(i) to teach the lessons implied in the above, and especially that of the true nature of leisure;
(ii) to provide a liberal education of the whole man, including his body (See Chapter 5);
(iii) to give opportunity for the release of his creative spirit;
(iv) to help him to discover and to use his own powers;
(v) to foster in him habits of independent and constructive thought.

2 D

It is notable that Aristotle should issue a warning of the dangers of over-athleticism in education, and no doubt he had Sparta in mind. He deplores any damage to the figure or any interference with the normal bodily growth because it produces an unbalanced or unrhythmical development. Those who are familiar with the ancient Athenian way of life know that appreciation of physical beauty was one of their first national preferences. This exaltation of the human form is seen in the Greek passion for personal beauty and physical strength, in the idealization, or, in some cases, the *idolization* of the athlete, and in the sculpture which developed its ideals as it watched in the Gymnasia the naked human form [1]. For the Jew, God made man in his own image; for the Greek, men made gods in their own image. On the other hand, Aristotle, in his *Ethics*, affirms that no man can be happy 'who is absolutely ugly', and that is why he places 'courage' first as a result of suitable physical education. We can accept this effect of physical education but we should not put it first. It is not upon the body, however, that over-athleticism has its worst effect; more serious is the effect on the *whole* man, the moral unbalance, a perverted sense of values, producing, as Aristotle says, 'young savages', than whom our 'flannelled fools' and 'muddied oafs' of the famous public schools are surely far more harmless. In any case, not all physical exercises necessarily foster courage. We should agree, however, that, for the most part, team games and Outward Bound activities do. Such physical exercises have other educational values of which Aristotle knows little or nothing.

To sum up; let it be granted that the most prominent element in the human make-up is the mind, and that educational practice hitherto has mainly consisted of a direct attack on the mind – the mind of the child as well as of the adult; but must we spend *all* our efforts on direct attacks on the mind by book learning and by academic methods? Could we not rather seek to outflank the mind by getting round the body, and not leave it, as hitherto, entirely to the hygienists and athletic trainers, who are excellent in their own fields, but often poor educators? This would mean giving the body a *liberal* education; and we could thus get at the mind less through the spoken word that enters by our ears, and *more by the skill that comes out of the five fingers*, and not only from these but also from the body as a whole. Then the body would be trained as a skilful community instrument both in work and in play – and more perhaps in play – for it looks as if the playtime of the people will be the great field where the new education must look for its conquests.

2 E

Aristotle devotes such a considerable amount of space to music in education that it seems to demand a chapter to itself. Moreover, he is clearly perplexed by the question, and the object of its teaching seems doubtful. But while he regards it as unnecessary compared with reading, writing, and gymnastics, he agrees that all children should cultivate the art. Of course, 'music' to the Greeks usually meant the accompaniment to song and dance, and was not thought of as independent of words or movement.

(i) In general, Aristotle sees its most obvious use for amusement and relaxation, but it is very important today not only as an active occupation for leisure but also as a recreation for leisure or occupation (in Aristotle's sense of the word).

(ii) He has no doubts, however, about the value of music in moral training. For him, as for Plato before him, tunes have implicit ethical qualities and the discrimination between them can stimulate ethical discrimination with a pleasure in the good derived from the pleasure of a good tune. We often speak of tunes, and especially musical rhythms, in ethical or semi-ethical terms such as 'noble', 'stately', 'soul-stirring', and the like, and say that we 'feel better' for having heard a certain musical composition. Is this, then, to be explained in terms of Aristotle's theory? If not, how? What he says about the *moral* effects of a trained musical discrimination is highly controversial, but such a discrimination in itself may be profoundly important in a time of abundant broadcast music, as an influence helping to form public taste.

(iii) As to the value of music in the cultivation of the mind, Aristotle does little more than hint at it and seems by no means clear about it. What are the purely intellectual effects of a musical training? Is there any significance in the not uncommon association of mathematical with musical ability? What should be the intellectual aims of music as a school subject, either for all or for selected pupils? These are questions to be dealt with in a later chapter.

3 · Who is Responsible for Education?

1 A

The relationship of father to son is regal in type, since a father's care is naturally for his children's welfare. The friendship of a father for his children is of the same kind as that of a king for his subjects, but here the benefits bestowed are greater, for the father is the source of the child's existence, and of its nurture and education. Paternal rule over children is like that of a king over his subjects, in virtue of the affection to which he is entitled by right of his seniority and maturity. Paternal authority has not the power to *compel* obedience, but law is the rule, emanating from a certain wisdom and intelligence, which *has* compulsory force. Paternal exhortations and family habits have authority in the household, just as legal enactments and national customs have authority in the State, and the more so, both on account of these ties of relationship and of benefits conferred which relate the head of the household to its other members. So he can count on this natural affection and obedience at the outset. Moreover, individual treatment is better than a common system, in education as in medicine. The best thing is that there should be a proper system of public regulation for education; but where the matter is neglected by the community, it would seem to be the duty of the individual to assist his own children and his friends' to attain virtue; but he will be more likely to succeed in this task if he has already acquired the science of legislation. Presumably a man who wishes to make other people better by discipline must endeavour to acquire this science, on the assumption that it is possible to make us good by laws (*Eth.* X, 9).

1 B

We must not regard a citizen as belonging just to himself; we must regard him as belonging to the State. There ought, therefore, to be laws which regulate education, and it ought to be conducted by the State. Moreover, the legislator should make the education of the young his chief concern. The constitution of the State will suffer if education is neglected, for the citizens should always be educated to suit their constitution. The whole of the State, in fact, has one common end, therefore the system of education must be one and the same for all, and its provision a matter of public action. It cannot be left, as it is at present, to private enterprise, with each parent making private provision for his own children, thus having them privately instructed as he himself thinks fit. Training for an end which is common should itself be common. So the nurture and education of the young should be regulated by law, since moderation and hardiness will not be painful when they become habitual. But it is not enough for the young to receive the right nurture and discipline at school; they must also practise the lessons they have learnt, and confirm them by habit when they are grown up. Accordingly, we shall need laws to regulate the behaviour of adults as well (*Eth*. X, 9).

1 C

The legislator ought to see to the provision of a stock of the healthiest possible bodies in our State nurseries, and therefore, the first attention must be devoted to marriage. This should not be contracted too early or too late in life – about eighteen years of age for women and thirty-seven for men – and the size of families should be limited. One of the primary duties of the legislator must be to root out the use of bad language so that the young may be kept free from both hearing and using it; he must also prohibit all statuary and painting which portrays any sort of indecent action. There are officials peculiar to certain States who concern themselves with keeping good discipline, as for the supervision of women, for enforcing obedience to the law, for the supervision of children, and for the control of physical education. The legislator, in short, must labour to ensure that the citizens become good men, and must know what institutions will produce this result (*Pol*. VII, 14 and 15).

[It will be remembered that Aristotle has already defined (Chapter 1, 1 B) virtue as a disposition of the mind, consisting essentially in the observance of the 'Mean', and it follows from the preceding sentence that it is the wise legislator who ultimately determines the mean.]

2 A

Aristotle makes much of the 'kingly' relationship between parent and child, which forms the natural responsibility of the father for the education of his children, and he sees clearly both the advantages and the disadvantages of this. The former are those derived from mutual affection and individual attention. The disadvantages are that paternal discipline can never have the impersonal and impartial authority of law, and that private education, in all its variety, will imperil the interest of the State. It must not, therefore, be allowed, except as a second best, and even then those responsible should have some training in the 'science of education'. Responsibility for education is therefore handed over to the State. In this connexion it may be of interest to note the comparison between Aristotelianism and the basis, both philosophical and political, of education in the Soviet Union. This similarity will be revealed to anyone who studies the observations accorded by some seventy American educationists who spent one month in the Soviet Union in the summer of 1958. These are summed up in a challenging volume entitled *The Changing Soviet School* [1].

> The Soviet system is a methodical plan for the education of all citizens. It stems from the confidence which can be traced back through Marx and Rousseau to Francis Bacon, that man, by the use of reason, can provide by legislation for all present and future social emergencies. Not only do the communists believe that their Party should have the power to legislate for social change, they also claim that it has the wisdom to determine what that change should be. Consequently, Soviet leaders claim to know what is good for everyone by way of education. By thus solving their philosophical problems they can concentrate on devising the best means to teach all Soviet citizens whatever they have decided to teach them . . . Somebody has said that if you have seen one Soviet school you have seen them all. There is some justice even in such a flippant dismissal of the issue. The uniformity of practice is remarkable. An almost intangible supervision on the part of the Central Committee of the Communist Party, guided by the educational research done by the Academy of Pedagogical Sciences, is all that seems to be required to insure uniform textbooks, priority for buildings, and an orderly flow of new school directors and teachers. This steel girding of the Soviet school is only superficially concealed by the outward decentralization. The best that can be said about government financing of education is that it is generous. . . . In fulfilment of the political goals, the schools have had considerable success

> in evoking commitment to communism. Not only are Soviet citizens as loyal to their government, as are serious citizens everywhere, but Soviet propaganda has convinced them that the government is *their* government. The occasional report of cynicism or apathy toward the regime tell only half the story; the 'right' values are quite effectively instilled in a substantial proportion, if not in a majority, of the pupils in school.

What is the situation today in this country? There is certainly a tendency of parents in the British welfare state to abdicate and to hand over all responsibility for the welfare (education included) of their children to the local education authority. Moreover, we note a growing readiness of the authorities to accept this. What, then, is gained and what is lost by this process of contemporary Aristotelianism, and, particularly, what is its effect on family life, juvenile delinquency, and the like?

Regarding the latter, it must be admitted that much of it appears to be due to lack of parental control and responsibility; that is to say, that the 'mutual affection' of parent for child, of which Aristotle speaks, has become, for a time at any rate, impaired. It may be that many parents do not realize how speedily their children 'mature', much more speedily in fact than was the case in *their* childhood. So it is that, when 'teen' comes to be added to 'age', the adolescent too often resents this 'parental control' and is prone to rebel against it. Wise parents, however, watching carefully the various stages in their children's growth, realize the moment when sympathy and companionship rather than control is what the growing child really needs. This is indeed the stage, from now onwards, when discriminating parents will take the growing child into their confidence more and more, bespeaking their *help* – and even their 'advice', when required.

If, however, the child does not respond to this treatment – and some clearly do not – the law, 'impersonal and impartial', steps in and some form of penalty or restrictive order is imposed, but 'what shall it be in the end thereof?'

On the other hand, are there not cases where the *parents* should be remanded, when it is proved, on convincing evidence, that they have made little or no effort to 'care for' their children? It is clearly wrong for the juvenile delinquent from such a family, and in such an environment, to suffer for his parents' sins of omission. Heredity and environment – what problems they present at the human level! Is it a case of 'visiting the sins of the fathers upon the children unto the third and fourth generation of them that hate Me'?

If there is any advantage in applying this rigid Aristotelian system to modern education, it may be found in the universal establishment of Comprehensive Schools for post-Primary children. This may result in the gradual extinction of class distinctions – socially if not intellectually. Have they succeeded in achieving this in Communist countries? We do not know yet; it is perhaps too early to judge.

2 B

The State, says Aristotle, is an educational institution, and ideally no private education, either by parents or other bodies, can be allowed. The sole responsibility for education and the sole authority for its conduct is vested in the State. Legislation is necessary for every detail of the educational process, including adult education.

Now when the Government-sponsored Committee for Education, as it was then called, took in hand the problem of the education of the masses in the middle of the last century, the sole responsibility for this, and the sole authority for its conduct, was actually vested in the State. Legislation was necessary for every detail of the educational process, even down to the details of 'payment by results'; and necessarily so, because it was an entirely new venture, and it was, therefore, not considered advisable to delegate any of its powers to Local Authorities, even though most of the schools already in existence were maintained chiefly by various Church authorities. Though we have moved a long way since those days, we cannot accept without qualification this doctrine of a central authority for the conduct of education and the ban of all educational institutions outside the State system; for our history and traditions are, on the whole, against it.

From this point of view the British case against complete State control of education has probably never been put more clearly and succinctly than in June 1965 by Dr Walter Hamilton, headmaster of Rugby, and that year Chairman of the Headmasters' Conference:

> To take away from such parents as at present have the means to exercise the right to educate their children at their own expense, if they choose to do so, would be an invasion of personal liberty unheard of west of the Iron Curtain, an act of tyranny which would not lose its tyrannical character because it was exercised by a constitutional majority.

Dr Hamilton then went on to state that most people would freely admit that

> Public schools ought to be widely accessible. There are many boys who for various reasons have a need, and particularly a need for boarding education, which we can supply and the maintained schools cannot.
>
> If the Secretary of State's intention for his educational trust is that it should establish assisted places in public schools on a substantial scale – and by substantial I mean something that might after a considerable period of time conceivably amount to something like half the intake of a school – I can say with confidence that he will find in both governing bodies and headmasters the greatest willingness, even eagerness, to cooperate.

Similar views have been expressed by many heads of independent boarding-schools, both for boys and girls, and we have every right, given our tradition of compromise between extremes – what was, in fact, Aristotle's mean – to anticipate the development of schemes which, while saving for the nation a form of education which has proved its distinct value over many centuries, will make such education available to a much wider range of boys and girls than those whose parents are able to pay the inevitably high fees.

Nevertheless, we have to take account of the tendencies since the Second World War for the State, even in the United Kingdom, to increase its direction of education. Examples are the 'control and direction' given for the first time in the 1944 Education Act, in the growing tendency of successive Ministers of Education or Secretaries of State for Education to exercise this control, with the resultant decreasing interest shown by some Local Education Authorities; in the attempts by the latter to recover their authority by taking over the proper responsibilities of the teachers; in the weakening of the Burnham Committee by the intervention of the Minister; by the prescription of religious instruction as a compulsory subject by the 1944 Act – the first time in this century that Parliament has 'interfered' with the curriculum; by the growing demand for the incorporation of all schools in the public system – particularly in certain political quarters; by the almost complete disregard of Section 76 of the Act, under which '*children are to be educated in accordance with the wishes of the parents, etc.*'. All this is pure Aristotelianism, but is it inevitable under the conditions of the modern welfare state? Should a campaign be conducted:

(i) for maintaining the proper responsibilities and independence of parents and teachers;
(ii) for preserving the independence of already independent schools, and designing a new status for them;
(iii) for resisting the improper intervention of a central authority, be it Minister or Parliament;
(iv) and for insisting that all educational measures must be based on the grounds of education, and not on purely political interests?

(i) This very desirable independence of parents and teachers, in the matter of education, might be brought nearer to fruition if there were greater mutual dependence on both sides. The valuable work of many parent–teacher associations is still often impaired by mutual embarrassment and suspicion. Parents, too often, assume that the upbringing of their children to a suitable intellectual and moral standard is the business of the schools; teachers understandably plead that they can accomplish nothing without parental support. Dr Michael Young, Chairman of the Advisory Centre for Education, has wisely suggested that the parents of children in Local Authority schools might be encouraged to take an active and practical role in the running of these establishments [2]. Mothers, for example, might be offered part-time jobs as auxiliary teachers invited to work on a paid or voluntary basis, as helpers in the playground or at meal times. Fathers might be asked to undertake small emergency jobs round the school premises, or even more ambitious enterprises, such as the building of a school swimming-pool – though these ideas might not always evoke immediate enthusiasm from the fathers concerned.

Paradoxically in the independent schools the case is different, and there is notably a much greater sympathy and understanding between parents and teachers. Is this because the parents are 'better educated'? (If so, why not adult schools for those who are not so 'well educated' – as in the Soviet Union?) Or is it that parents who pay for the education of their children are anxious to see that their teachers 'deliver the goods'? Be that as it may, if the same sort of feeling could be engendered in the Local Authority school parents, if they could be brought into regular and informal contact with the schools, it would be all to the good. The aim of all this, to bridge the gulf between parents and teachers, is a worthy, and even an urgent, one. No doubt the combined pressure of these two groups on public opinion would make the way clearer for maintaining their proper responsibilities and independence.

(ii) The preservation of independence for our recognized independent schools is another object well worth contending for, as it is closely connected with the right of parental choice specifically granted by the 1944 Act.

Suppose all our schools were integrated into the State system what should we *lose*? For some time past the independent boarding-schools, as a whole, have possessed certain advantages over the Local Authority and Direct Grant schools; namely, by their smaller classes, by better equipment, *especially* for the Arts, and by much greater opportunities for cultural pursuits, while many of their less fortunate opposite numbers are wasting time travelling backwards and forwards by bus, coach or train. 'Hotbeds of Snobbery'? For the most part not so, and increasingly not so, as more and more local authorities are paying the fees of pupils who are deemed to be up to a certain agreed standard of attainment, and, of course, whose parents so desire it – but how many of these, even in these days, 'dread the thought of boys and girls going away from home'? These, however, are the very schools where so many thrilling experiments are carried out, the results of which gradually filter through to other, less independent, institutions. We hear also a great deal about some of the so-called crank schools, often looked askance at by the authorities, but, in point of fact, they have taught us much about the psychology of children at school, because their pupils are usually few in number, and they have had both the time and inclination to explore educational methods more fully than others. We should therefore, lose much by integrating these and all other independent schools into the State system. Perhaps the whole problem might be solved when every town in the country has a school of the type of Christ's Hospital in its boundaries!

(iii) and (iv) are really closely related to the problems raised by (i) and (ii) and can be solved only by converting public opinion to more enlightened views on the subject. To sum up: Aristotle's doctrine depends on the conception of a common end, demanding a common education, which, for the present, we are not ready to accept without qualification. It also implies the belief that a people can be educated and made good by Act of Parliament, which is clearly untrue.

2 C

The educational legislator must concern himself with:

(i) prenatal eugenic measures for the maintenance and improvement of the stock; and in this connexion Aristotle makes a reference to the necessity for State nurseries;

(ii) the censorship of art and literature for children, as well as of their companionship;

(iii) determining what institutions most successfully educate good men.

(i) Is this suggestion part of our answer to the problems of the educationally sub-normal child, as also of Special Schools in general?

Since the turn of the century much remedial work has been set in motion, but much more remains to be done – by Local Education Authorities, and by the teaching profession rather than by 'charity'; for in the case of the latter there seems to be a good deal of *overlapping* still, to the detriment of some equally deserving causes. As the State is responsible for the education of its citizens – with the reservations already discussed – it should surely be responsible to the same degree for the repair of the defects of their minds and bodies. 'Charity', both for the dispenser and the recipient, might well be more effectively expended on the many voluntary societies which clamour for some form of social, *personal* service.

In the matter of overlapping in the Special Schools themselves, Dr Mary Wilson, President of the Association for Special Education, had some pertinent comments to make in her presidential address at the 27th Biennial Conference of the Association (1964):

> Our main purpose during the next few days is to consider the points at which the work of various professional groups overlaps. . . . It is not surprising that many people who have come into special education with a genuine desire to help handicapped children should so often find themselves at variance with colleagues who seem to have other ideas of how the children can best be helped. . . . If we look closely at the development of special educational treatment in this country, especially since the war, one notable feature has been the extension of non-teaching provision made within the education service as well as the greatly extended contacts outside. It is now quite usual for a school for physically handicapped children to be regularly

> visited, not only by the School Medical Officer, but also by consultants interested in each of the main disabilities. In addition to a full-time nurse on the staff there will probably be physiotherapists and speech therapists in regular attendance, nursery assistants, general attendants, and bus attendants who provide physical care are in close contact with the children, and often form relationships which cannot be ignored. In schools for maladjusted children a recognised part of the provision is psychiatric consultation, psychiatric social work with families, periodic examinations by an educational psychologist, and quite often psychotherapy within the school itself. . . . In boarding schools we may have all this with, in addition, a house staff whose main duties resemble those of parents rather than teachers. . . . In all these fields there may be people who consider themselves to have a special responsibility towards a particular child, and there are very few who would not claim to be interested in the 'whole child'. It can be complicated when, in addition to the child's parents, there are at least three different people each saying 'This is my patient, my case, or my pupil', and none of them understanding what the others are doing. A good case can be made out for more social workers attached to schools, particularly for educationally sub-normal children [3].

The speaker went on to discuss the various 'meeting points' to be found in special education, and described the overlap between education and therapy as one of the most 'fascinating'.

As to the respective limit of ages for marriage proposed by Aristotle – eighteen years for women and thirty-seven for men – because of the need to secure, as far as it is humanly possible, conditions for fruitful marriages, the disparity of the extremes seems somewhat larger than we should concede today. At any rate, it suggests that Aristotle was taking into consideration the physical fact that women, on the whole, mature earlier and age more quickly than men, and therefore that men should normally be older than the women they desire to marry. In the matter of the limitations of families, to which he refers, we have our Marriage Guidance Councils, which are evergrowing in number and esteem. We have also our contraceptives, oral and other. On the other hand, to a Greek, childlessness was a far greater misfortune than it is with us. Euripides, for example, in his drama *Ion*, puts children before wealth and royal palaces, and there are many similar preferences to be found throughout the pages of Greek literature. Hence Aristotle's anxiety for the maternity clinic for married women.

(ii) The matter of censorship is with us a very controversial question, and must, if it is to be meaningful, cover not only books and pictures, as with Aristotle, but also films, radio, television, and, presumably, statuary. Any kind of censorship is practically non-existent, as it is certainly out of favour. It would be generally agreed, no doubt, that the Athenians were no prudes. They did not affect a mock-modesty – that attitude of extravagant propriety, which might be described in much more unflattering terms, such as is affected by so many Europeans today. Else why is it that a certain newspaper which specializes in accounts of unsavoury stories from the Courts has a larger circulation than any other newspaper in the country? In Ancient Greece both men and boys stripped naked for playing games, and there is yet no reason to suppose that they were more given to homosexuality than many Europeans today. Have *we*, on the other hand, gone too far in the direction of release and freedom? Any attempt to impose a direct censorship would not only be extremely difficult but would also be hotly resisted, and would probably do more harm than good; but are there any indirect means which might be used?

As far as the censorship of the Press is concerned there exists a Press Council, which, in spite of its readiness to take what positive action it can, receives only occasional attention *from* the Press, mainly, of course, from those members of it who are generally not guilty of any offence. But, at least, it is duly constituted, and does take cognizance of offensive or ill-advised behaviour on the part of the newspaper world as a whole.

The television authorities, of course, manage their own censorship, such as it is, and dramatic scripts are presumably reviewed by the Censor of Plays before public performances of them are permitted. As far as children are concerned, very little is at present known about their reactions to the television screen, as a whole, though most of the educational programmes are certainly above reproach from the moral standpoint. But nowadays many children are permitted to stay up later than formerly, and it is in the more adult-viewing programmes that the doubts of many thinking parents begin to arise. Here again a body like a school parent–teacher association, linked up with other such associations all over the country, could wield a strong moral influence over public opinion in the matter of urging restraint and common decency in all pictorial representations, whether in the Press or on the screen. Or, if this fails, does this country need some great prophet, another Wesley, for example, to recall its people to a sense of true moral values?

The Report of the Committee on Broadcasting (1960), though not exactly up to date, does contain some pertinent comments, not so much on schools' programmes – which are generally favourable, but on the wider implications of television viewing as a whole. Thus the Association of Education Committees has this to say:

> We are especially concerned with the influence of television on younger people and on children. It is, we believe, important to recognise that it is not enough to produce programmes suitable for children between the hours of 5 and 6 p.m. In fact, the proportion of children viewing between 6 and 9 p.m. is higher than the proportion of adults in the general population viewing between these hours. We submit that programmes during this period must be suitable for *family viewing*, and must have full regard to the fact that young people and children constitute an important part of the audience.

And again:

> We are appalled at the let-down not only in standards, but in the assumption that adults or near-adults are happy not in living in terms of their own best values, but in terms of values that the lowest common denominator of attracting mass audiences will inevitably produce. . . . It is the complete and insulting contrast to the values implicit in a good school that our young pupils are nightly exposed to in programme after programme. It is not enough for I.T.A. or programme companies, or even aggrieved B.B.C. to say that this programme of violence or that of banal triviality cannot be proved definitely to have lasting harmful effects on those who placidly watch. It is not that we have a lofty or idealised conception of what life in a civilised community can be: it is rather that the purveyors of mass communications are acting as though they held the belief that we must needs love, or, at least, go on watching the *lowest* when we see it.

The National Union of Teachers, which also contributes to the Report, appears to be of the same opinion on the question of television's influence on children:

> The Union is aware that certain statistical research has tended to minimize the allegedly bad effect on children of some programmes. It must accept the validity of this work, but it remains unconvinced that the figures give the whole of the story, or that the whole of the story can ever be elicited by sociometric techniques of the sort used. There are imponderables in the mind of the individual and in the collective ethos of a society, and it is hard to accept that constant subjection to the presentation of values that seem to be

debased and unworthy does little or no harm to either; at all events teachers are not prepared to take that risk if they can see means of avoiding it [4].

(iii) This gives the legislator complete control over the type of school to be allowed. What if he decides that independent schools outside the State system are desirable?

Aristotle is right in describing the State as an educational institution, and it is becoming progressively so with us. Indeed, it is impossible to evade its frequent exhortations, through the Press and radio for example, to 'live a good life' if not in Aristotle's sense of the phrase.

These exhortations cover a good deal of ground: for health and hygiene, for education, for more careful car-driving, for the avoidance of litter, and for greater efficiency in household affairs – to name only a few. The State, in fact, is a teaching State, and the question arises, how far is it effective as such? We must note the growth of sexual licence, the increase of crime of various kinds, the tendency to assess 'worth' (*virtus*) in terms of money and possessions rather than as an estimate of personal character; and, not least, the hideous hiatus which exists for the great majority of our adolescents between school-leaving and any form of further education.

There are also certain forms of pleasure, such as drinking and gambling, harmless in moderation, which, in recent years, have shown a considerable growth in their excessive use. The picture is not overdrawn; statistics are not necessary to prove the veracity of it. All this is common knowledge. On the other hand, there was probably never a time when the problems of education stood out more strongly in the limelight than they do today, not only in this country but in the world around; and this must imply dissatisfaction and discontent with things as they are. But, whatever the results of such deliberations as dissatisfaction may bring about, whether they come in the 1970s or a century later, it would seem that we, and our successors, have much to learn from the thought of Aristotle, though his problems were much simpler, and the dimensions of his city-state much smaller.

4 · The Process of Education

(*Recapitulated from Chapter* 3, 1 B, *for further consideration*)

1 A

It is difficult to obtain a right education in virtue from youth up without being brought up on the right lines; for to live temperately and hardily is not pleasant to most men, especially when young: hence the nurture and the exercises of the young should be regulated by law; for temperance and hardiness will not be painful when they become habitual. But it is not enough for people to receive the right nurture and discipline in youth; they must also practise the lessons they have learnt, when they are grown up. Accordingly we shall need laws to regulate the discipline of adults as well.

These are the general aims which ought to be followed in the education of childhood and of the *stages of adolescence which still require education.*

The sort of people which a legislator can easily guide into the way of goodness are those with a natural endowment which combines intelligence and spirit. When they have that endowment, the rest is entirely a matter of the education which he provides; and they will learn it partly from a training in habits, partly from a system of instruction.

Youth never resents being governed, or thinks itself better than its governors; and it is all the less likely to do so if it knows that it will have to take over the government on reaching a proper maturity. In one sense, therefore, it has to be said that governors and governed are the same sort of persons; in another, that they are different. The same will be true of their education; from one point of view, it must be the same; from another, it has to be different, and, as the saying goes, 'If you would learn to govern well, you must first learn how to obey.' This means that a good deal of the work which is generally accounted menial may none the less be the sort of work which young freemen can honourably do – if they have been taught what the 'spirit of freemen' means (*Eth.* X, 9).

I B

The reproduction of the species sometimes issues in children of 'poor quality', who are beyond the reach of education; moreover, there may be persons who cannot possibly be educated or turned into good men. If the legislator ought to see to the provision of a stock of the healthiest bodies in the Nurseries of the State, there should be a law to prevent the rearing of deformed children. If, however, children are then conceived in excess of the limit, as fixed by law, miscarriage should be procured before sense and life have begun in the embryo.

Pregnant mothers should pay attention to their bodies, in that they should take regular exercise and follow a nourishing diet. Their minds, unlike their bodies, should be kept free from exertion. Children's physical powers, too, will be seriously affected during their growth by the nature of the nourishment provided for them. It is evident that a diet abounding in milk is best suited to their physical development, and the less wine they are given, the better. It is also good to encourage every sort of physical movement which their little bodies can make; to habituate them to the endurance of cold from their earliest infancy. This greatly conduces to their general health, as well as hardening them in advance for military service. Whenever it is possible to implant a habit in children it is best to begin the process of habituation in their earliest years, and then to increase it gradually (*Pol.* VII, 14).

The next stage of the child's life, which lasts until the age of five, is one which cannot admit of any set lessons or compulsory tasks, for fear of hindering its growth. But it is a stage which leaves room for some practice in movement, to prevent the body from becoming limp; and this should be provided by games as well as in other ways. These games should be neither laborious nor effeminate, but such as become a freeman. Care should be taken by the Superintendents of Education to determine the sort of tales and stories which children of this age ought to be told. All these things should prepare the way for the occupations of later years, and even the games of children should be representations of what later will be activities of real life. Plato, in his *Laws*, would like to prevent young children straining their lungs and sobbing, but thinkers of this sort are wrong in the view they take of this matter. For it helps their physical growth; for it is, in its way, a sort of physical exercise. Indeed, just as adults, when holding their breath, acquire strength for exertion, so children are strengthened by straining their lungs. The Superintendents must also exercise a general control over the way in which children pass their time. In particular they must see to it that very little of their time is passed in the company of slaves. The stage of life during which children pass up to the age of seven is bound to be one of home-training, and, young as they are, they will be likely to contract vulgar habits from anything vulgar they hear or see. (Censorship of language, painting, and the like, has already been alluded to in Chapter 3.) The means required for achieving general excellence are natural endowment, habit, and rational principle, and the first has already been dealt with (Chapter 1). It now remains to consider the other two means, and to determine whether training in habit, or training in rational principle, i.e. mental training, ought to come first. The conclusion is obvious. Children's bodies should be given attention before their minds, and their 'appetites' should be given attention before their souls. But the regulation of their 'appetites' should be directed for the benefit of their minds, just as the attention given to their bodies should be intended for the benefit of their souls. In educating children we must use the instrument of habit before we use that of reason, and we must deal with the body before the mind. We must, therefore, begin by putting them into the hands of physical instructors and games masters. The former will give them a proper habit of body; the latter will teach them all the necessary techniques and accomplishments. Till the age of puberty the physical exercises should be light, and there should be no rigorous dieting or violent exertion, such as may hinder the growth of the body. When that age has been reached, the next three years may be spent in other studies, the next stage of development being properly given to hard exercise and strict diet. It is not right to do work with the mind and body at the same time, for the two different sorts of work tend naturally to produce different, and, indeed, opposite effects. Physical work clogs the mind, whereas mental work hampers the body. There should be two different periods of regular education – the first from the age of seven to that of puberty, and the second from puberty to the age of twenty-one. Those who divide man's life into seven-year periods are, on the whole, right. On the other hand, the divisions which we ought to follow in education are the divisions made by Nature herself. The purpose of education, like that of Art in general, is simply to copy Nature by making her deficiencies good (*Pol.* VII, 15).

2 A

For Aristotle the educational process begins in infancy with an early habituation to temperance and toughness, and continues till the age of twenty-one, with regular education starting at seven, the division between Primary and Secondary falling at the stage of puberty. There is only one hint of further education, contained in the phrase 'The stages of adolescence, which will require legislation.' There is no programme of higher or university education, and no reference to adult education. We have to consider, therefore:

(i) whether Aristotle was right in fixing the age of seven as the starting-point of school life, and what there is to be said for raising *our* school age limit from five to six or seven;

(ii) what Aristotle would have said about courses in, and selection for, higher education. Would he, for example, have followed Plato's lead (and it must be remembered that the *Politics*, as it has come down to us, is unfinished) and, if so, what light can that shed on our problems of admission to universities, university courses, and technical colleges?

(iii) how can we fill up the gap which Aristotle leaves for adult education?

Before considering, as a whole, the educational process as Aristotle views it, we cannot fail to notice these important omissions; but more light is thrown on the details of these by Plato, both in the *Republic* and in the *Laws*. One question then arises as to the relationship between the views of these two great philosophers on the whole subject of education, although it is generally agreed that, in the main, there was substantial agreement between them. The other question is, how far Plato's views in the *Republic* were modified by those in the *Laws*, which was a work of his old age. It is said that he was much discouraged by the course of events at this time, and by the reception of his previous book. None the less, it seems that he had not really changed his ideas as to what was true and important, though he did make certain concessions to the weakness of human nature – or shall we say the *Laws* represented a more practical approach to education than he had favoured in the *Republic*?

As to the first question, it will be generally agreed that Aristotle imbibed many of his basic philosophical ideas from his former master, Plato, especially, for example, the view that education means 'loving the right things, and hating the things one should hate', and furthermore the connexion between happiness and goodness, which is the theme of Aristotle's verses on Plato. (*Fragmenta*, ed. Rose, no. 673). Judging from the similarity with which they both prescribe for children in their earliest years it may be presumed that Aristotle would have followed the main lines of Plato's system, for the later stages of education, especially as the latter had advocated in the *Laws* the spread of education throughout the whole community of citizens, instead of confining it to the governing class of philosophers as he had done earlier in the *Republic*.

(i) If we were to raise the age of school entry to six or seven years, it would certainly release a number of teachers for work in Primary Schools, and, at first sight, would solve some of our most pressing teacher-shortage problems. But it would also necessitate the provision of a number of Nursery schools to cater for the growing number of children whose parents go out to work. Ideally the older age of entry might be an educationally sound move, but the administrative difficulties involved would make it almost impossible in present circumstances. Yet we must consider the current regulations for the education of Infants in other countries in Western Europe, and decide whether they have anything to teach us in this important matter. In Scandinavia, for example, where the climatic handicap to young children is considerable, compulsory school attendance does not begin until the age of seven. There is an interesting passage in the brochure issued by the Swedish Ministry for *Foreign Affairs* which describes the working of the New Primary School Statute, issued, no doubt, partly for the consideration of *Ministries of Education* in other countries:

> The period of compulsory school attendance starts from the beginning of the autumn term in the calendar year when the child reaches the age of seven. After medical examination and other tests the child, if found fit to be ready for school, may, subject to the permission of the School Board, be admitted to a Primary or Experimental School one year earlier. In Sec. 15 of the new

> statute there is a new provision to the effect that a private school may not accept children below the lower age limit for compulsory school attendance without the permission of the Municipal School Board. *The reason for this is that the development of the child may be harmed if it goes to school before it is ready to do so* [The author's italics].

There is another aspect of Scandinavian hesitation about early schooling that is worth consideration – consideration which may be forced upon this country as a result of shortage of single women teachers of infants aged five to seven, namely, the half-day system. In Scandinavia the school day is not, for the early years, a 'full' school day from 9 till 3 or 3.30, as it is with us, but just the morning. This enables married woman teachers who have children of school age to teach in the classes of the very little children, and to have nearly half a day looking after their home and family. It is also adequately long enough for most small children, for they find the excitement of mingling with a large group tiring, and to be quiet at home in the afternoons is beneficial to them. Indeed, in England, mothers frequently find that little children, especially in the first year of infant school, return home not only exhausted but fractious as a result of their nervous fatigue and prolonged restraint during group activities. The suggestion that such half-day schooling for infants should be introduced experimentally is by no means new. Indeed, in July 1961 Mr Peyton asked the Minister of Education in the House of Commons if, in view of the fact that in most European countries education is not compulsory until a child reaches the age of six years, he will consider making attendance optional until a child is six years old. During the same session another M.P. suggested that parents who felt strongly about the matter should have discretion to keep a child under six but over five at home in the afternoons so that the start to school is not quite so sharp and absolute as it is at present. More recently, among the main recommendations prepared for a report to the General Advisory Council for Education under the Chairmanship of Lady Plowden, we find the following:

> Part-time schooling should be compulsory from the age of five years with the possibility of full-time attendance, if desirable. Full-time compulsory education should not begin before the age of six years [2].

Let us suppose that a system of half-day schooling between the ages of five and six or even between the ages of five to seven would be in the best interests of the children, what other advantages would accrue to it? It would certainly help to release a considerable number of teachers over the country as a whole, which might automatically allow of smaller classes here and there. And – most important of all – it might discourage the mothers of small children from engaging in whole-day work. Could not such a scheme be tried out in some small County Boroughs, in which the Local Education Authority and local industry might well co-operate, in order to test its validity?

(ii) More light is certainly thrown by Plato than by Aristotle in the *Republic*, and in the *Laws* as we have already noted, on the process of education, by stipulating clearly the length of time allotted to each stage; he begins with a primary course up to eighteen years, and this, as we learn from the *Laws* (809 *seq.*), is subdivided as follows:

(*a*) ten to thirteen years (when the more 'serious' stage of education begins), military lessons and exercises, and, of course, reading and writing, while 'music and gymnastic' are the main studies throughout the whole course of the Primary stage;

(*b*) thirteen to eighteen years, 'cyphering', carefully chosen literature, science, and especially astronomy, mensuration, and geometry, in the early stages with material things;

This is followed by four divisions between the years of eighteen and fifty:

(*c*) eighteen to twenty years, military service, and physical training;

(*d*) twenty to thirty years, a course in higher arithmetical studies for those capable of it;

(*e*) thirty to thirty-five years, a course in Dialectic for the same;

(*f*) thirty-five to fifty years, public service in subordinate posts.

He adds that there must be appropriate *tests* of physical, moral, and intellectual qualities at each stage. Thus one of the principal aims of higher education, according to Plato (*Republic* Bk. 7), must be the production of the rulers of the State, and these, the embodiment of knowledge and wisdom, will always be few, and will be the product of higher education. In another passage in the same book he repeats this statement, with the important addition that such guardianship of the State, and management of social affairs, is within the powers of women as well as of men; both, therefore, should receive the same education.

With regard to *our* problems of admission to universities and university courses, Plato's 'tests', such as they are, do not afford much help. It would seem that such tests as were devised for higher education were of a moral and psychological nature – 'for the voluntary abandonment of bad opinions and for the retention of right ones'; indeed, this was one of the aims of 'science' teaching. This all savours too much of brain-washing and McCarthyism for modern minds to accept.

At any rate he does suggest specific means in his system of education for ensuring 'the right attitude of mind' for passing these tests:

(*a*) by a life which includes hardship and pain', that is to say, a disciplined life, in which things must be done whether they are liked or not – the antithesis of a 'free discipline';

(*b*) 'by exposing the young to temptations', which presumably involves the choice of friends and a certain degree of *laissez-faire* in the matter – shades of Farrar's *Eric, or Little by Little*!

(*c*) 'by keeping the attention fixed on the things that matter' in the classroom, to avoid wishful thinking and to foster intellectual integrity.

Moreover, in his summary, Plato expresses mainly similar opinions on education to those we have already observed in the writings of his pupil. For 'if the right people are to be chosen, the tests must be open to all, and there must be equality of opportunity in education'. Heredity is accepted in the intellectual and moral spheres, as well as in the physical (*Republic* 415), but not as an absolute law. All of which suggests the possibility of transfer from school to school to ensure equality of opportunity (End of Book 3).

Tests for admission to places of higher education today vary considerably from one university to another. At the present time there are two main groups, the colleges of Oxford and Cambridge in one, and the 'Provincial' universities in another. The former are still the most sought after, the reasons for this being numerous; but their long unbroken tradition is probably the one that counts for most. The requirements for admission to all universities, however, are, on the whole, similar, but in the new ones the problem of supply and demand is greater because of the considerable number of candidates involved. For such subjects as divinity, Greek, and music, for example, the demand would probably be small and the chance of gaining admission proportionately greater. There is, therefore, no small variation in the grades of 'A' levels required, though normally three of these is the target set for admission. This raises the question of admission to the more 'popular' courses, for which the demand is greater. A partial answer to this is the Universities' Central Council for Admission, which acts as a clearing house for all these universities, by receiving all the application forms and passing them on to the universities concerned; the main purpose being to ensure, as far as is possible, that all vacant places are filled, and that a candidate's choice of subject should be taken into consideration. It should be added that into this U.C.C.A. the universities of Oxford and Cambridge have recently been integrated.

(iii) The gap which Aristotle leaves for adult education is one which, in spite of the gallant efforts of various voluntary organizations such as the Workers' Educational Association, and Local Education Authority's Evening Institutes, has yet to be filled. For adult education is the consummation of the whole educational process according to the 1944 Act, and one which becomes more, and not less, significant with the improvement in the general system of education. At present, however, only a very small proportion of the population is involved; yet it is a part of education which is becoming increasingly important, as Aristotle would no doubt have recognized, with the increase of leisure time available.

The main purpose of the Act is stated in its opening paragraph:

> to promote the education of the people of England and Wales, and the progressive development of institutions devoted to that purpose, and to secure the effective execution by local authorities, under his control and direction, of the national policy for providing a varied and comprehensive educational service in every area.

Finally, and specifically in the matter of 'further education' the Act determines that

> it shall be the duty of every Local Education Authority to secure the provision for their area of adequate facilities for further education, i.e.:
> (*a*) full-time and part-time education for persons over compulsory school age; and
> (*b*) leisure-time occupation, in such organized cultural training and recreative activities as are suited to their requirements, for any persons over

compulsory school age who are able and willing to profit by the facilities provided for that purpose (Para. 41).

and

Not later than three years after the date of this part of this Act, it shall be the duty of every Local Education Authority to establish and maintain County Colleges . . . for providing for young persons who are not in full-time attendance at any school . . . such further education including physical, practical, and vocational training, as will enable them to develop their various aptitudes and capacities, and will prepare them for the responsibilities of citizenship (Para. 43).

(*a*) It shall be the duty of the Local Education Authority to serve upon every young person residing in their area who is not exempt from compulsory attendance for further education a 'College attendance notice', directing him to attend at a county college, and it shall be the duty of every young person upon whom such a notice is served to attend at the county college named in the notice;

(*b*) The requirements specified in a college attendance notice shall be such as to secure the attendance of the person upon whom it is served at a county college –

(1) for one whole day, or two half-days in each of forty-four weeks in every year he remains a young person (i.e. until 18 years of age), or

(2) for a continuous period of eight weeks in every year (Para. 44) [3].

The first serious attempt in the right direction, in this country at any rate, seems to have been the Day Continuation School, which appeared for the first time in the London County Council area, as well as in a few of the larger provincial towns, in the year 1919. These developments were in fulfilment of clauses of the 1918 'Fisher' Education Act which empowered local education authorities to open Day Continuation Schools for boys and girls at work under the age of sixteen (to become eighteen after seven years).

The main object of these schools was to absorb the many young people who had recently left school – at fourteen years in those days – including many who had played truant for many weeks before they were fourteen, and to give them something to think about beyond their various jobs; for most of them, in 1919, had had no difficulty in finding them, demobilization having scarcely begun. They had to attend the school, which was often poorly housed in some disused Institute building, for two periods of four hours a week; but, in the following year, when the results were beginning to look most promising, the continuation schools which were being attended voluntarily were closed and only those attended by certain young government employees, the General Post Office for example, were retained. Had the government of the day had the courage to make the establishment of these schools all over the country compulsory instead of permissive, they might have planted a seed the fruits of which we might be enjoying today and our England, in the meantime, would have been a better and a more productive community, especially during the tragic decades of unemployment and the dole, 1920–40.

It is generally thought that the whole scheme was 'killed' by 'Big Business'; at any rate, letters poured into the Press prophesying the disaster to trade if the existing schools were allowed to continue to function, and certainly if the scheme became nation-wide! And an 'economy' campaign, strongly sponsored for months by one of the Press empires, urged reduction on educational and other social expenditure and eventually had its effect on the government. So this section of the 1918 Act was allowed, like the similar section of the 1944 Act subsequently, to become a dead letter.

What a contrast is found in Germany during the same years! The 'berufsschulen' (i.e. day-release trade and professional schools) which had been so greatly developed in Munich by Georg Kerschensteiner that they had been copied in many parts of the country, were now made compulsory for all young workers under eighteen [3*a*]. So almost every young worker all over Germany, within a few years of the end of the First World War, was attending school one day per week having, during that day, four lessons related to his work and four of general education, including civics and often aesthetic subjects and physical education. For girls the general education always included domestic science, which in Germany embraces child care and upbringing.

In France, too, the end of the First World War was followed by upsurge in the education of the young worker and the 'Loi Astier', often called 'The Charter of Technical Education' was passed in 1919. The provisions of this Act included compulsion upon employers to adjust the hours of work of all employees under the age of eighteen so that they could attend several hours per week, sometimes admittedly in late afternoon, in relation to their work and the wider knowledge and increased general knowledge that advance and promotion in their line of work would entail. For every type of work involving the acquisition of skill and knowledge a national 'Certificate of Professional Aptitude' was devised, with an examination which was almost entirely practical and all young workers were encouraged to prepare themselves for this test over a period of three or four years. As the C.A.P. was recognized by Trade Unions and industry for wage advance this was, and is, a great incentive. To pay for the cost of the study classes the French Government, under the Loi Astier, imposed on every employer an 'Apprenticeship Tax' representing a very small percentage charge on his total wage and salary payments. It is noteworthy that this is the basic money-raising principle of the Industrial Training Act passed in the United Kingdom some forty-five years later!

Prior to the final shaping of this Act, however, some arguments had been put forward by one or two pressure groups to the effect that young workers ought to be allowed to opt for day-release for technical studies. A committee appointed by Sir David Eccles, then Minister of Education, reported that if this right were granted there would have to be so much extension of facilities for technical education that other educational developments would be held back, since no additional educational expenditure could be envisaged.

Following upon this report the Henniker-Heaton Committee was set up by the Minister of Education in November 1962 to consider what steps should be taken to bring about the maximum practicable increase in the grant of release from employment to enable young persons under the age of eighteen to attend technical and other courses of further education. On the publication of their report 'Day Release' in the spring of 1964 the Association of Teachers in Technical Institutions (representing 20,000 teachers) announced that it was very disappointed that so little progress would be completed by 1970, and stated that it would publish a fuller statement at a later date.

Thus in the autumn of 1964 the Association published a Commentary on the Report, the Introduction to which runs as follows:

> The Association must record quite categorically its bitter disappointment that so little progress should be contemplated by 1970. It has never accepted the argument that compulsory day-release would strain teaching resources or national finances to such an extent as to be unattainable by 1970. The 1944 Act promised one day a week release for all young people under 18 not in full-time education. We feel bound to state our view that to suggest a target

of day-release for considerably less than half of this group of young people a quarter of a century after the passing of the Act, and to aim at attaining that figure by methods of persuasion that have not hitherto been outstandingly successful, represents a major failure of our society to face its responsibility to the rising generation. Such a failure can only result in a lowering of the human, social, and economic potential of the working lives of the young people who ought to have been able to profit from the education that is now not going to be made available to them. All young persons should be entitled by law to receive further education, and in our experience measures to secure day-release will never be effective if they are based on exhortation alone. It is essential that they should be backed by positive legislation.

As a contrast we should consider the most significant recommendations of the Henniker–Heaton Report, namely, Nos. 1 and 11. Thus No. 1 recommends

> that for 1969–1970 a national target should be set of at least an additional 250,000 boys and girls obtaining release from employment for further education. Our aim involves an average increase of the order of 50,000 a year during the next five years. It results in roughly doubling the present numbers.

And No. 11 which recommends that

> Employers should devote practical attention to the further education needs not only of those to whom priority must be given, but of all their young employees, girls as well as boys. This would be in the interests both of the young people and of the employers themselves [4].

'*All* their young employees, girls as well as boys' includes the less academic, now conveniently known as the 'Newsom young people'. In a paper entitled 'Prospects for the Newsom Boy' delivered at the British Association on 1 September 1964, by D. M. Downes, a Lecturer of the London School of Economics, the speaker made the following very important remarks:

> By the term 'Newsom boy' we mean the 'Jones' and the 'Robinsons' – the two middle and the lower quarters of the secondary modern age-group as assessed by reading ability – and not the 'Browns' – the top quarter in ability as assessed by reading tests, who are really grammar school boys manqués, who go on much more frequently than the rest to white-collar and skilled manual jobs, day-release and apprenticeships, and who are more likely to be middle-class in origin. To what extent do Newsom boys, by this definition,

participate in further education? A study carried out by Peter Wilmott in Bethnal Green earlier this year gives a pretty representative picture. Of 148 boys aged 15–20 who had been to secondary modern schools, including a few who had been to comprehensives, 55% had had no education since leaving school at 15; 26% had experienced or were undergoing some form of day-release, and 19% some form of evening-only education. The 1964 Henniker–Heaton Report on day-release similarly showed that 28% of boys aged 15–17 and not in full-time education were granted some form of day-release. These figures are, however, misleading, for they take no account of courses discontinued, failure rates and non-attendance. The wastage in evening-only education is especially severe, amounting to almost 50% by the end of a course. Obviously, these figures come nowhere near implementation of the section of the 1944 Education Act which calls for part-time compulsory education for all till the age of 18.

Developments *since* the Crowther Report strengthen the view that there is very little prospect of any radical improvement in the voluntary F.E. system in the foreseeable future. What has happened since Crowther is that education is becoming more stratified, not less, and these trends show up exceptionally clearly in the further education field. We are moving towards a meritocratic system catering for four broad, but clearly distinct strata, with tremendous inequality in the investment of resources at each level. At the top we have the expanded elite, catered for by the Robbins Report, and in turn meant to cater for our needs for administrators and technologists. The next stratum is the apprenticeship layer, at present covering the bulk of skilled workers, and now extended upwards to take in technician grades. These two strata practically accommodate all boys of middle-class origin and above, if we include black-coated workers with apprentices. The third layer is largely prospective, designed to make up for the inadequate numbers in the second layer, and overlapping considerably with it. The third layer takes in those skilled workers and top-level semi-skilled who are not accommodated by the creaking apprenticeship system, and who are to be catered for by the Industrial Training Act 1964 and the Henniker Report proposals for doubling numbers in day-release over the next five years. This layer has yet to emerge, but will do so in response to our need for more skilled labour. The fourth layer constituting over 40% of the 15–17 age-group, is simply the rest, perhaps a third of whom will, in a decade, constitute an unemployable rump, unless rapid and radical changes are made to their prospects and education at both secondary and further levels [4].

It is to be hoped that the announced plan of the British Government to raise the school-leaving age to sixteen in 1970 will indeed be carried out, and that the changes stimulated by the Schools Council, and by other bodies, in the curriculum for the Newsom boy will have become common practice by that fateful educational year.

If not, the prophetic warning in the last sentence quoted above will be well on its way to fulfilment.

But even when the school-leaving age is raised to sixteen the need for day-release education will be no less than it is today. In the economic and social situation lying ahead everyone must continue to learn for the greater portion of life and nothing can be more harmful to the young worker than an abrupt ending of learning when he leaves school.

While we do not go so far as the examination candidate at a northern College of Education – 'when a youngster is about to leave school his school must try to make him realize that learning does not stop when he leaves school, but only starts' – we must regard some part-time attendance at some form of College of Further Education as the normal course of events, at least to the age of eighteen.

But, to return to the main subject of this chapter – the process of education – Aristotle makes the significant remark that education works on a 'natural endowment of intelligence and spirit'. And, although we are not absolutely clear what he means by 'spirit' in this context ('courage' or 'enthusiasm', possibly, e.g. what we call a *spirited* response to a challenge), there is no doubt that some attention must be paid to natural endowment in framing a varying educational programme to suit the needs and capacities of children in general.

Now that the 'catastrophic' 11+ examination is almost in the limbo of history, other more sound and less hurried methods of discovering the spectrum of a child's abilities are taking its place. And the curriculum of Comprehensive Schools, whether of the one-tier or two-tier systems, has been constructed to allow as far as possible for the whole gamut of abilities, aptitudes, and interests. Thus we now have, in a great number of the nation's secondary schools, under the same roof pupils who a few years ago would have been divided into types, i.e. 'Grammar', 'Secondary Modern', and in some areas 'Technical'. For those pupils who, in the past, would have been called 'Grammar School' types, the most weighty examinations, at least for some years, will continue to be the General Certificate of Education at 'O' and 'A' levels, especially the latter. But for those who show lower academic aptitude by the age of fifteen, but still need a 'paper qualification', the Certificate of Secondary

Education will undoubtedly prove an attraction and give motivation for increased intellectual effort. Moreover, the opportunity which is afforded under the regulations of the C.S.E. for examinations to be school based and externally moderated gives scope for the development of new and exciting syllabuses geared to the real needs and interests of the less academic pupil. In its Examination Bulletin No. 5 the Schools Council gives guidance for the development of this more difficult, but far more rewarding, method of both assessing and encouraging achievement among secondary school pupils. In its Examination Bulletin No. 1, the Schools Council had challenged teachers to develop new syllabuses in the school subjects:

> The C.S.E. examinations are not to be regarded as watered down versions of the examinations at the Ordinary level of the G.C.E., nor is it intended that they should be used as selection tests for entry to G.C.E. courses. The two examination systems must be free to develop in their own ways according to the needs of the majority of pupils for whom they are designed. And in many subjects, though not necessarily in all, this will mean that the two systems ought properly to adopt different syllabuses, and to assume different approaches to teaching. Where this is so, it will always be wrong to enter pupils for the same subject in both examinations in the same year, and it will normally be difficult to justify using the C.S.E. examinations as a trial run for G.C.E. examinations in the following year [though, no doubt, many will be tempted to attempt the second alternative!].
>
> The Council recognize, however, that the existence of two overlapping systems will involve the schools in difficult choices, and they are therefore anxious to make apparent the overlap that will exist in terms of the *calibre*. [i.e. degree of personal capacity, weight of character, etc.].

There are five grades in the C.S.E. examination – Grade 1 describes a standard such that the candidate might *reasonably have secured a pass* at Ordinary Level of the G.C.E. examinations, had he followed a course leading to that examination. Grade 4 describes a standard of performance expected from a candidate of average ability who has followed an appropriate course of study in the subject. After Grades 1, 2, 3, and 4, Grade 5 is simply described as a 'standard within the scope of the C.S.E. examinations below that of Grade 4', and performances below Grade 5 are unclassified [5].

All this involves serious consideration being given to natural 'endowment of intelligence and spirit' in those who possess it as well as in those who do not. In other words, there should be equality in education, but not identity; equal opportunity, but varying provision. This enlightened opinion of Aristotle, though he does not develop it at all, is one which would be whole-heartedly accepted by our educational experts today.

'Learning to rule and be ruled', and the practice needed in both, is part of the educational progress. In a small State like Athens the incentive 'to rule and be ruled' was very strong; for 'it was necessary for many reasons that all should share alike in ruling and being ruled'. It has been estimated that the free adult male population of Athens in the fifth century B.C. numbered only 30,000, and of these no less than 1,900 would be chosen by lot (but seldom, if ever, re-elected) to fulfil various offices in the State, both great and small in the public administration. So 1,900 places of office would be open to the whole body of citizens approximately once in every sixteen years, that is, twice in every generation [6]. And so a nation thus engrossed, day by day, in the details of its own government, must necessarily be experiencing a process of education.

As far as our schools are concerned, allusion has already been made to the possible value of Senior Councils or Committees in assessing the degree of culpability in their unruly school-fellows; but in a few of our schools such councils are elected by their fellows to formulate a code of rules for the conduct of the school as a whole. This is one way, at any rate, of experiencing the democratic way of life, provided that personal animosities, with all the injustice they often engender, are forgotten. The really important point about them is that such Councils should be real and effective if they are to be used at all for these purposes. For modern youth (*pace* Aristotle) does resent being governed, or at least, being governed as it is at present, without any chance to express an opinion, still less to bear any responsibility. Even the opportunities for voluntary community service are very limited. But probably modern youth would be more ready to accept government if it could both recognize and respect the authority and reason behind it, and see these as based on rational principles and common sense.

Also, can it be considered *reasonable* to withhold the vote from young men of eighteen when, in the event of war, they would be called up for military service at that age? Despite the fact, now generally accepted, that youth matures a good deal earlier than in former generations, we are slow to recognize it in terms of the suffrage. Again, can it be denied that in most spheres of occupation there is little opportunity for them to obtain posts of responsibility until they have reached the age of at least thirty, and, in some fields, middle age? Of course, an earlier suffrage implies an earlier training of the reason than Aristotle allows for. But television, radio, film, programmed instruction, and language laboratories have made such training both possible and necessary.

Finally, the 'menial tasks' to which he refers are presumably, for us, the 'chores'; which are an accepted part of modern education, even if they are not always performed in the 'spirit of a freeman'.

2 B

The process of education begins with pre-natal measures to safeguard the health of the mother, with which we should agree in principle, though some of their details are questionable. The number of ineducables must be reduced as far as possible, and the legal limitation of the family involves the exposure of the weak, and legalized abortion. These were, apparently, the normal methods by which the Greece of those far off days, 'the survival of the fittest' was achieved. One explanation of the need for these summary measures may be found in Aristotle's direct allusion to the prospect of future military service and future occupations, even at the infant stage. For us, the problems of the educationally sub-normal, physical, moral, and intellectual, are in process of being dealt with.

No doubt much of what Aristotle has in mind for the infant stage is already being done in our Nursery Schools, of which the prototype has already been given us by Plato in the *Republic*, physical exercises, no set lessons, and mimicry – up to the age of five. He amplifies this by describing young children as 'born imitators, and therefore must be given, in their education, the right parts to imitate'; hence the importance of censorship for all undesirable deeds and words. It is unfortunate, but quite natural, that he also disparaged imitations of manual or industrial occupations by children, because it shows that he was evidently blind to the effects of manual training on the mind and character, especially for the development of self-expression and self-confidence (witness a lad engrossed in a hopeful job of carpentry). Certainly our modern conception of the 'dignity of labour' which ultimately can be traced back to Christ the carpenter, was far removed from the minds of both these great philosophers. This denigration of 'labour' in Aristotle's view may have been due to its connexion with slavery, and all the restrictions and frustrations which the term implied. Moreover, manual labourers worked such long hours that their bodies often became deformed by disorder and disease over a long period of years; and such physical deformities were, as we know, anathema to the more cultivated members of society.

The process of education, therefore, and the agents in effecting it are, according to Aristotle:

(*a*) training of the body by physical education;

(*b*) the control of the appetites – the non-rational part of the soul – by habit;

(*c*) the growth of reason – the rational part of the soul – by teaching; but is meant ultimately for the mind.

Physical education instructors are to be used for giving children a correct habit of body, and games masters for the necessary physical skills. Here it may be suggested that Aristotle:

(i) postpones straight teaching and the training of the reason far too late;

(ii) has very little idea of what physical education means, and, in particular, of its non-physical effects;

(iii) carries out an unreasonably sharp division between the physical and the intellectual, with his fantastic 'sandwich courses' and in consequence fails to educate the *whole man*.

(i) In Aristotle's day, when the physically and mentally sub-normal seem to have been, for the most part, 'disposed of', it would seem that he does indeed postpone the training of the reason unduly, though the importance to the Athenian of physical perfection, from the earliest stages, as we have already observed, must always be borne in mind. In our day, of course, there is no such universal priority of training for the one or the other; a child's 'natural endowment', whether great or small, will indicate a just proportion between the two.

(ii) But still, the fact remains that Aristotle had very little idea of what true physical education really means, and, in particular, of its mental and moral effects. But our greater understanding in this field is very modern and it is only a decade or two ago that the long-accepted term 'Physical Training' gave way to its more appropriate title of physical *education*. Even so, research in this subject has hardly begun and there is probably a very great deal waiting to be discovered regarding the relationship between the mind and the body and the nutrition of both.

Indeed, Plato held a more enlightened view of the whole subject than his pupil. For him (*Republic* 403–12) the relation of mind to body is a compound one, and neither can be treated in isolation. If the body is overtrained at the expense of the mind the result will be mere athleticism or valetudinarianism; if *vice versa*, an effeminate intelligentsia will emerge; for 'Man is a soul using a body'. A good mind will ensure that the body receives due attention – neither too much nor too little, the mean in fact, and, therefore, influences the whole man for good. On the other hand, a good body helps to ensure the good mind, with a healthy outlook on life, and even a sense of responsibility. Moreover, under the same terms Plato includes sense-training, to see and hear with acuteness, for example, and manual training, to develop the skill of the fingers; for 'Man', as Carlyle says 'is a skill-hungry animal'.

And these principles are the very ones which modern schemes of Physical Education are engaged in putting more widely into effect. They may be summarized as follows:

(*a*) their comprehensive character;

(*b*) their relation to other school work and activities;

(*c*) the choice of exercises to foster alertness and concentration;

(*d*) their method of teaching in small groups, with due attention to the individual, especially in cases of physical retardedness, together with opportunities for training in leadership;

(*e*) close co-operation between the Director of P.E. and his colleagues;

(*f*) the inclusion of manual dexterity; and

(*g*) opportunities for sex education.

The cumulative effects of such a training are likely to be an increased mental alertness, better carriage – grace, poise, and balance – for girls as well as for boys, and the development of courage, self-confidence, and self-respect.

Perhaps the Platonic view of 'Gymnastic' may be summed up, not in the somewhat trite phrase *Mens sana in corpore sano*, but in another,

Man is a soul using a body. In other words, *sanitas* in one is impossible without *sanitas* in the other. Such, according to Plato, at any rate, should be the process of education as far as Physical Education is concerned.

5 · The Instruments and Content of Education

I A

Pol. VIII *passim* Opinion is divided about the subjects of education. All do not take the same view about what the young should learn at school, either with a view to plain goodness, or with a view to the best life possible. Nor is the opinion clear whether education should be directed to the understanding, or mainly to the training of moral character. There can be no doubt that such useful subjects as are really necessary ought to be part of the instruction of children, though this does not mean the inclusion of every useful subject. Occupations are divided into those which are fit, and those which are unfit for freemen. Thus the total amount of useful knowledge imparted to children should never be large enough to make them mechanically-minded. The term 'mechanical' or machine-minded (*banausos*) should properly be applied to any occupation, art or instruction which is calculated to make the body, or soul, or mind, of a freeman *unfit* for the pursuit and practice of goodness. We may, accordingly, apply the word 'mechanical' to any art or craft which adversely affects man's physical fitness, and to any employment which is pursued for the sake of gain, and keeps men's minds too much, and too meanly, occupied. Much the same may be said also of the liberal branches of knowledge. Some of these branches can be studied, up to a point, without any illiberality; but too much concentration upon them with a view to obtaining perfection is liable to cause the same evil effects that have just been mentioned. Indeed, a good deal depends on the purpose for which actions are done or subjects are studied. Anything done to satisfy a personal need, for example, or to help a friend, or to attain goodness, will not be illiberal; but the very same act, when done repeatedly at the instance of other persons may be counted menial and servile.

It is clear that there are some branches of education which ought to be studied with a view to the proper use of leisure in the cultivation of the mind. It is clear, too, that these studies should be regarded as ends in themselves, while studies pursued with a view to an occupation should be regarded merely as means, and not matters of necessity. This will explain why our forefathers made music a part of education. They did not do so because it was necessary; it is nothing of the sort; nor did they do so because it was useful, as some other subjects are.

We may take it as evident that there is a kind of education in which parents should have their sons trained, not because it is necessary, or useful, but simply because it is liberal and something good in itself. To let youth run wild in savage pursuits, and to leave them untrained in the discipline they really need, is really to degrade them into vulgarity.

I B

In educating children we must use the instrument of habits before we use that of reason, and we must deal with the body before the mind. For there is now general agreement about the necessity of physical training, and about the way it ought to be given. Till the age of puberty the exercises should be light, and there should be no rigorous dieting or violent exertion such as may hinder the proper growth of the body.

Reading and writing are useful in various ways – for money-making, for housekeeping, for the acquisition of knowledge, and for a number of political activities. Drawing may be held to be useful in helping men to judge more correctly the works of different artists. Music serves none of these uses, nor does it resemble physical training in any way, which improves health as well as preparing pupils for military service. It has no visible effect upon either. We are thus left with its value for the cultivation of the mind in leisure. This is evidently the reason for its being introduced into education; it ranks as a part of the culture which men think proper to freemen.

A training in music should include some share in its actual performance. We must begin by noting that the purpose for which the young should join in the actual performance of music is only that they should be able to judge it. This means that they ought to practise the execution of it in their earlier years; but it also means that they ought to be released from it at a later age, when the education they have received in their youth should have made them able to judge what is good, and to appreciate music intelligently.

The study of music should be pursued in such a way that it will neither impede the activities of later and riper years, nor produce a 'mechanical' habit of body which is ineffective for the purpose of the period of military and civic training – ineffective, that is to say, in bodily exercise, and in the pursuit of knowledge. Moreover, pupils should not be set to work on the sort of performances which are the feature of professional competitions. In other words, they should not be made to attempt the extraordinary and extravagant feats of execution which have recently been introduced into such competitions, and have thence passed into education. Even so, performances should only be carried to the point at which students are able to appreciate good melodies and rhythms. Pipes* should not be used in musical education, and we ought to avoid any other instrument which requires professional skill, such as the harp, and all other such instruments. The instruments which ought to be used are those which will make the student intelligent, whether in the field of music itself, or in other fields of study. A further argument against the pipe is the fact that it does not express a state of character, but rather a mood of religious frenzy. Therefore it should be used on those occasions when the effect to be produced on the audience is the release (*catharsis*) of emotion, and not instruction.

Another reason against the use of the pipe in education is the fact that pipe-playing prevents the player from using his voice. Many older instruments, too, were rejected by our ancestors – those calculated merely to please the audience, and all others requiring merely manual dexterity. The goddess Athenē invented the pipe, but later threw it away in disgust, because of the ugly look on her face when she was playing it; but, more likely, because the study of pipe-playing had nothing to do with the mind. Thus, both in regard to the instruments used, and the degree of proficiency desirable, we may reject any

* See pp. 86, 87.

professional system of instruction, that is to say, any system intended to prepare pupils for competitions.

We accept the classification of melodies into those which are expressive of character, those which stimulate to action, and those which evoke inspiration – and there are musical modes corresponding to these classes.

When education is the object in view, the modes which ought to be used are those which express character best. Thus, since the Dorian mode stands to other modes in the relation of a mean, it is the one which suits the young best as an instrument of education.

1 C

A man who wishes to make other people better by discipline must endeavour to acquire the science of legislation – assuming that it is possible to make men good by laws. For to mould aright the character of any and every person who presents himself is not a task which can be performed by anybody, but only, if at all, by the man with scientific knowledge, just as is the case in Medicine and the other professions, involving a system of treatment, and the exercise of prudence. Not only is this scientific knowledge required but also practical experience as well as study (*Eth.* X, 9).

2 A

Aristotle's underlying principle in all this discussion is that there should be nothing 'mechanical' about the processes of teaching and learning, and that the 'mechanical' is anything which fails to fit the student for the life of a freeman, and for the pursuit of goodness.

Here again, in the context of those occupations 'which are unfit for freemen', we may fittingly recall some of the handicaps in the lives of some of our own countrymen; the long hours of work in many cases making a man's body ill-proportioned, with some muscles over-developed, and others neglected; the pneumatic drill worker deafened, the tailor and the cobbler slip-disced, the worker in slate and sandstone quarries prone to silicosis – to mention only a few. Is it too much to hope that, in the near future, these 'living tools' may be replaced by 'inanimate' ones so that they may be more fitted to live the life of a comparatively 'free man'. Meanwhile do *we* find our teachers still tied and bound, like these 'living tools' already mentioned, to a number of outworn dogmas of pedagogy?

It is not, however, so much a question of *what* subjects should be included in the curriculum, as of *how* they should be taught and learnt, and the effect of this teaching and learning. In all teaching, especially of the arts and of physical education, the teacher not only imparts information and stimulates discussion about the subject but also conveys some measure of his personality to the class, enriching the subject by his own personal powers of inspiration. Such a teacher is, in a very true sense, an 'amateur' – a lover of his subject, and, not only of his subject but also, in a strictly Platonic sense, a 'lover' of his pupils as well. 'Platonic affection' is the phrase derived from the concluding sentences of Plato's *Symposium*, in which Plato was extolling the fatherly interest that Socrates took in his young pupils. Such teaching is what Aristotle seems to describe by the word 'liberal', which is his appropriate epithet for the teaching of the 'expert amateur'.

Those, on the other hand, who undertake the art of teaching as a task to be executed with the least possible inconvenience to themselves, or, in the world of today, solely with a view to enabling their pupils to pass an examination, and not as a vocation, are what Aristotle describes as mere 'professionals'. It is the teacher himself who can make a subject liberal or the reverse.

Aristotle also makes the profound point that the most liberal subjects on paper can become the most 'mechanical' in fact, if the degree of specialization or concentration is over-exaggerated. Even Latin, still regarded in some countries of western Europe as the key subject of a liberal education, may be so taught as to add nothing to the development of the pupil's perceptions regarding the use of words, the expression of feelings and the ways of transmitting thoughts.

In the light of this principle we should consider:

(i) whether *all* curricula, if properly taught, have not got in them the makings of a liberal education;

(ii) what is the real significance (if any) of the sharp distinction which some people still make between a technical and a cultural education;

(iii) the 'mechanical' effects of our pre-occupation with examination results;

(iv) the illiberal effects of a high degree of specialization, even on a liberal subject in the sixth form.

(i) Ideally, no doubt, in the hands of the liberal-minded teacher many subjects in the curriculum of the technical colleges may include the makings of a liberal education as well, as, for example, in the beauty of the machine, in mathematical expressions, and proofs, or in the design and form of common tools and articles of daily use. On the other hand, have not some forms of art already borrowed from the technical field some of its geometrical ideas with which to portray the human form both in painting and statuary?

This distinction between 'liberal' and 'illiberal' education which underlay all Greek thinking on educational values, was most clearly and explicitly expressed by Aristotle (1A). In later centuries, there was a tendency to confine the liberal arts for the study of freemen to the following: grammar, music, geometry, arithmetic, astronomy, and certain aspects of rhetoric and dialectic – seven in all. This conception of seven liberal arts or branches of knowledge was to have considerable influence on education in western Europe, as in England during the Middle Ages, and well nigh down to the eighteenth century, with recurrent modifications, of course. These arts were called 'liberal' as opposed to those trades and skills practised for economic purposes by slaves or by persons without political rights.

By the thirteenth century, however, there came a redistribution; these seven liberal arts had been divided into two groups: the first, known as the *Trivium* (place where three ways *meet*) included grammar, dialectic, and rhetoric; the second group, called the *Quadrivium* (place where four ways meet) included arithmetic, geometry, astronomy, and music. In passing, it is interesting to note that the very derivation of these two latin words suggest a fusion of the subjects in each group.

From the sixteenth century and onwards logic dropped out of the *Trivium*, having been relegated to the academic courses at the university; and in the grammar schools the *Trivium* was ultimately reduced to the study of the classical languages, and this alone thereafter provided the basis for a liberal education.

In the last century wider conception regarding education began to take shape; for Matthew Arnold, reporting to the government on secondary education in a number of continental schools, especially those in France, declared that

> the idea of a general liberal training is to carry us to a knowledge of ourselves and of the world around us. We are called to this knowledge by special

aptitudes which are born with us; the grand thing in teaching is to have faith that some aptitudes of this kind every one has. This one's special aptitudes are for knowing men (the Humanities); that one's special aptitudes are knowing the world – the study of Nature. The circle of Knowledge comprehends both, and we should all have knowledge of the Humanities; but he whose aptitudes carry him to the Humanities should have some notion of the phenomena and laws of nature. Evidently, therefore, the beginnings of a liberal culture should be the same for both.

More specifically, perhaps, in 1926, Professor Whitehead has stated the case for this integration of curricula in the following words:

There are three main methods which are required in a national system of education, namely, the literary, the scientific, and the technical. But each of these curricula should include the other two. What I mean is that every form of education should give the pupil a technique, a science, an assortment of general ideas, and aesthetic appreciation, and that each of these sides of his training should be illuminated by the others. Lack of time, even for the most favoured pupil, makes it impossible to develop fully each curriculum. Always there must be a *dominant* emphasis. The most direct aesthetic training falls in the technical curriculum in those cases when the training is that requisite for some art or artistic craft. But it is of high importance in both a literary and a scientific education. . . . The problem of education is to retain the dominant emphasis, whether literary, scientific, or technical, and without loss of co-ordination to infuse into each way of education something of the other two [1].

(ii) The sharp distinction between the technical and liberal sides of education, which existed in this country almost up to the time of the First World War, is gradually disappearing. For, in the Victorian age at least, with all its social snobbery, cultural and technical education, on the whole, stood at poles apart. Any truck with the latter was regarded by our middle-class forefathers as something unclean and unbefitting a 'gentleman' – 'banausic' Aristotle might have called it – and their sons were normally discouraged from having anything to do with it. But as wars consistently bring great revolutionary changes in their train, so in England and, previously, elsewhere, technology, so essential in war, came to be regarded as equally essential in times of peace. So it earned the status of 'Culture' as in the Technische Hochschulen of Berlin, of Zürich, Delft, Stockholm, Massachusetts, New Orleans, and finally in 1965, in the technical universities in the United Kingdom. In all these institutions, though technology occupies the centre of the stage, the aesthetic subjects, and modern languages, and the social sciences all have their place. So, too, in the United Kingdom today, liberal studies as well as technical ones, are found in every technical college of every level, whether regional, area, or local. Moreover, as these two aspects of education and their relationships become more and more the subject of lively discussion both in Parliament and in the Press, the greater is the likelihood of seeing them in their *ultimate* relationship.

(iii) The preoccupation with details of examination results is an ever-present temptation to those of us who have to do with them, and one of its effects is to regard the whole procedure as a cast-iron ('mechanical') system which can never go wrong.

It is true that, in a world where so many examinations count for so much, we cannot remain placidly unconcerned with their results; but, if, as seems to be quite reasonable, a more general use of books of *reference* (relevant to the particular examination, of course) were permitted to the candidate, in advanced studies especially, the examination itself would prove more of a test of 'intelligence', initiative, and creative thinking, than of memory alone. In these cases the preoccupation with examination results should not be so compelling; for those with the keenest brains, their abilities already recognized through the daily work, would almost automatically succeed. There is the familiar story, perhaps apocryphal, of the student, endowed with a photographic memory, who could reproduce on paper almost anything he had read, and so, in one sense 'knew all the answers'. In his *viva voce* after the written papers, it was found that he was totally unable to describe what it was all about! Needless to say he was not granted a pass. If there is any truth underlying such stories we have justification for the oral examinations which play so large a part in school assessment in the Soviet Union and in some examinations in Scandinavia.

(iv) Deep specialization even in liberal subjects in sixth form work may be just as 'illiberal' in effects as exclusive courses in various branches of science for the depth and the demands on time can narrow the student's interests, restrict his sympathies and give him a false sense of superior wisdom. But, as a result of much deliberation on the matter, there is now much more give and take between the sciences and the humanities. Indeed, it may be stated without fear of contradiction, that the aim of our more discerning leaders in the field is the education of the whole man.

For example, it is the view of Sir George Pickering, Regius Professor of Medicine at Oxford University, that specialization starts at an absurdly early age. 'Poor little devils,' he said, 'they have their minds warped from the start. Fancy having to choose your sixth-form course at 13.' Blaming university requirements, Sir George said he thought the most important thing that could be done would be to end the evil at one stroke. As Oxford and Cambridge were now getting the selected 'best young minds of the nation' they must be prepared to provide the intellectual leaders of tomorrow. So the universities should be taking note of what the problems would be. Society now needed generally educated men and women. He did not regard as 'educated' an engineer who could not write English nor speak a foreign language; nor people who did not know the elements of modern science. 'I would therefore like to see something like the requirement of one Arts subject at 'A' level, and one Science 'A' level as a condition of admission.' 'Undergraduates,' he suggested, 'should have both the interest and the leisure to attend lectures in subjects in which they were *not* going to be examined. That would be extremely difficult *without school preparation in these subjects*.' (Author's italics) [2]. So the challenge is passed to the schools.

Educational Guidance

What is more important, however, is that boys should know exactly what examination they need to take in view of their future careers; and the relevant question may well be asked, does early and intense specialization *channel* boys into certain types of career, or, indeed, cut them off from a whole range of careers? For there can be no doubt that preselection into scientific and non-scientific fields takes place by the age of fifteen. Is this too early for such a vital decision to be made? And do boys actually have a career in mind when they choose their 'A' level examination subjects? The replies to the questionnaire dealing with choice of 'A' level subjects and choice of careers (prepared by the Oxford University Department of Education in 1963) throws some light on the problem. The most optimistic interpretation of the fact that some 44 per cent of the boys chose careers to fit in with their 'A' level subjects is that, since these subjects are the 'best' or 'most interesting' for the boys concerned, the careers should likewise prove to be suitable and interesting. However, as the boys' experience of the various fields of study, and of life, is so inadequate at the time when the 'A' level course is decided upon, it is likely that many of these boys are caused to take up careers for which they are not really suited. Not infrequently during interviews boys commented that they did not take the right subject examinations for some particular career. It is noteworthy that in the 'List of Recommendations' (para. 225) in the Robbins Report the following occurs (No. 4):

> Institutions of higher education and the schools should consider how better information can be made available to young people and their parents about the courses available for higher education [3].

But to return to the curriculum, which Aristotle divides into necessary, useful, and liberal subjects, can we accept this analysis as valid for our purpose in curriculum building? In other words, does it give us a *principle* to guide us in the choice of subjects? The importance of having such a principle is obvious; but, for the most part, our curricula, in the United Kingdom at least, (except for the three R's) have 'just growed' in reluctant response to changing popular demands, and other such ephemeral circumstances. Aristotle's basis may be reconciled with our three A's (age, ability, and aptitude), if we add 'the pupil' to each of his three categories. In doing this, we should prescribe as necessary subjects for all learners the Dialectic, that is, learning how to think; Grammar, that is, the means of understanding other people's thoughts; Rhetoric, that is, the means of expressing one's own thoughts. These formed the *Trivium*, the basis of the medieval curriculum, already described, which had to be mastered as the necessary tools of learning before the pupil passed on to the more specific subjects of the *Quadrivium*. So a contemporary version of the medieval *Trivium* as the stock in trade of all schools up to the age of approximately thirteen is what is needed. Much of this would, in fact, be covered by the three R's and other conventional subjects – but only if these were taught with this special purpose in view. This significant slogan, 'How you teach is more important than what you teach' is no product of modern thought, it is in fact one of Aristotle's fine inspirations.

'Useful' subjects would be useful either for occupation, for citizenship, or for leisure, and could be partly the same for all, or at least for the great majority of pupils, and would partly vary with individual needs. Aristotle admits these 'useful' subjects but says little or nothing about them. From our point of view they would be useful either directly, in the form of technical education, for example; or indirectly, for the purpose of examinations which open the way to occupations, the G.C.E. for example. The White Paper 'Better Opportunities in Technical Education' (1961) foreshadowed considerable changes in the length and content of part-time courses for craftsmen and technicians (ages 15–18). It suggested that when courses were lengthened to the 330 hours per year recommended in the Crowther Report (1959) the time given to English and General subjects, including physical education, should be increased. It also referred to the need for 'experiments into the form in which general studies can best be introduced into courses for this type of student, and into the best methods of teaching them'. The Working Party on Re-organization of Part-time Technical Courses therefore appointed an Advisory Committee which was asked to draft notes for the guidance of technical colleges on the arrangement for, and treatment of general studies when part-time technical courses are lengthened to make approximately 90 hours per year available for them. They are based on the assumption that some 2½–3 hours per week are available for these studies.

Among the suggestions for the widening of horizons and the development of personal interests were the following:

> Man and Nature – the universe and man's place in it, e.g. men and machines, culture and civilisation; the arts – music, literature and the drama; the crafts – practice of handicrafts; physical education and recreation.
>
> The purpose of the scheme is to awaken, stimulate, and nourish interests, and to make the students aware of the opportunities in the college and in their local community for taking these interests further and onward into adult life. They should be made aware of and introduced to local societies, clubs, the Youth Service, centres of further education and interest groups of all kinds [4].

Education for Citizenship

In this matter which was discussed in Chapter 2, the ideal was seen to consist in 'Education *about* democracy', which was to be achieved by the pupil in his school 'doing the actions by which a democracy will be enabled to survive'. Now the school is a society, and this fact is of special importance in these days of increasing individualism. Should not the school be regarded as an epitome of the great world around, fostering a national unity, bridging gaps, and developing a community sense even where communities tend to be very large – as in the Comprehensive Schools, or at Eton College? Should it not teach a contributory, rather than a grasping, patriotism as a conception of world-citizenship? The truly democratic ideal may be based on the corporate life of a school, where master, prefects, and rank and file are each doing their own job. Is not this an indirect education in national unity and citizenship, especially when posts of responsibility are multiplied to a reasonable degree; and direct teaching through history is added?

The above reference to world-citizenship opens up a matter of supreme importance in its relation to education. Under the umbrella title of 'Tomorrow's citizens' the Council for Education in World Citizenship a few years ago held a conference in London to discuss the whole problem of education and peace, and the following notes cover some of the points of permanent importance discussed at it:

> What responsibility have educators for introducing young people, rooted in one ideology, to the concepts and practice of others, and for doing so in a sympathetic way? If to do so means that a teacher must suppress his personal beliefs, have we the right to expect this in the cause of international understanding? Can we teach toleration?
>
> In considering what contribution education has to make to international understanding we have, in the past, laid special responsibility on certain subjects in the curriculum. History is one of these. For if we must examine the past in relation to the present, should it not include the history of other peoples and races seen in ways other than as related only to the history of our own country?
>
> Increasingly also, geography is emerging as a subject which provides a vehicle for those reaching towards international understanding. As the fundamental importance of the effect of physical environment upon man becomes apparent, so geography becomes a study of man and his development and even moves into the field of history. Can the subjects remain separate and water-tight in today's world?
>
> Since the Second World War there has been a notable increase in the number of international festivals of the arts, in the exchange of orchestras, opera and ballet companies, and in travelling art exhibitions. The successful presentation of any of these may engender a warm, pleasant feeling of appreciation, but have they no direct contribution to bring to this particular area of human endeavour?

If such questions can reasonably be asked about the arts, is it not even more justifiable to pose them in relation to the sciences? Have the sciences, as they are taught in schools, any contribution to make to education for international understanding? How much attention do the social sciences, for example, receive in our schools?

Again do the mass media, through the Press, radio, television and cinema, in the final analysis, play a greater part in influencing our attitudes towards other peoples and nations than the educational process carried out in schools?

What does it all add up to? Is race tension and prejudice any less real as a result of educational effort? Will foreign affairs figure at all prominently in British General Elections because we have a slightly better informed electorate? The answer to both these questions is probably 'no'. This is partly because the developments mentioned previously, though impressive, have still not affected the great mass of schools. But is it reasonable to consider that they may one day become an integral part of our everyday educational practice, so that education becomes concentrated upon the production of a 'world citizen'.

And so the C.E.W.C. carries on its vital 'missionary' work for a deeper international understanding, in close co-operation with the United Nations Association, commended by all men of goodwill, and speaking to the youth of this country through the pages of its companionable magazine *World* (a monthly publication). For it is to youth that its appeal comes most cogently and resolutely [5].

Community Service

But there is a further development of these ideals which should not be lost sight of – the obligation of personal service, for senior pupils at any rate, outside the school. For many years past, many of the Public Schools have been sponsoring 'School Missions' for the benefit of their less prosperous young fellow-countrymen and women in the 'sub-standard' quarters of London and the larger provincial cities. This has proved more valuable when resident settlements have been established than when sporadic visits are paid to a number of boys' clubs – visits which nowadays are often regarded with the suspicion that they are made mainly 'to see how the poor live'. But the generous motive which prompted such enterprises must not on that account be disregarded, much less despised. On the contrary, they are moves in the right direction, though some of those to whom the boys are keen to 'minister' are prone to be reluctant to 'surrender their independence'. Would it not, therefore, be more desirable for a school to plant its settlement or 'mission' in the town or city *nearest* to it, so that contacts could be more regular, and meetings more informal? Indeed, with the social and economic changes that are continuing to fray the edges of class stratification, and the projected raising of the school-leaving age, we need to think more in terms of class co-operation than in terms of 'slumming', however well-intentioned.

This social outward-looking movement among adolescents in our schools appears to be growing apace. In one London area, for example, some nineteen schools are involved, in varying degrees, in helping the elderly and the lonely. In the summer of 1964 a clearing house in the area was established, to which both local and statutory bodies could refer cases suitable for adolescent service – to avoid overlapping. The names of old people who needed help were thus passed on to the schools and youth clubs. In one direct grant school in London about one-third of the girls participate in such 'relief works' as painting, decorating, home visits, shopping, repair of radio sets, etc. From another school the girls go mainly in groups of two and three for about two hours a week to visit the local almshouses in the area to render the same kind of assistance. They also provide musical evenings there in the form of Chamber Concerts and Carol Services. Another school – a Comprehensive one – is divided into four Houses, each of which gives practical help in some good cause, e.g. animals, the blind, children, and old people. At this school, too, many of the pupils are socially handicapped, difficult, and often bitter, and rebellious; but the teaching staff see this voluntary service as a vital link in helping such girls to overcome their deep sense of feeling unwanted – their sense of restlessness, in fact. Pupils in a North Country mixed High School are combining for a work-camp project in East London – and so the good work goes on. But a more comprehensive list of examples of such service is to be found in the King George's Jubilee Trust pamphlet, entitled *Opportunity for Service* [6]. Moreover, conferences on the subject are arranged periodically by the National Council of Social Service [7].

As has been already observed, the young should be educated not only as individuals but also as co-operative members of a Society.

> Among the broadening conceptions dominating modern education, none is more significant than that which recognises the child as a social being, with claims beyond those met by a curriculum in ordinary academic studies. These

two requirements, parts of one whole, when considered as one, will effect an expansion of communal life and interests of the young, which we are seeking to achieve for them. And so the best forms of communal life will be fostered by an education which regards social activities as a medium for the development of the higher qualities of individuals, rather than as something to which the individual development must be subordinated. By grouping for some common purpose a boy may lose some of his personality, but gains in his serviceability to his group [8].

Education for Leisure

A liberal education for leisure, as an end and not as a means, is something 'good in itself'. It is, as Ruskin pointed out long ago, in itself an advancement in life, and not *for* advancement in life. But subjects are not absolutely good in themselves; they are good relatively to the needs of the pupils, and at this stage the pupil's choice must be the determining factor. Nevertheless, he will need guidance and an ample field in which to make his choice. This means that, if schools are to make adequate provision for education for leisure, there must be a considerable increase, particularly at the senior stages, in both subjects and activities. Have we as yet begun to think in liberal enough terms about this? Aristotle speaks about the 'proper use of leisure in the cultivation of the mind', and, in evaluating such subjects and activities, we might well pay attention to this, and consider its significance today. What is equally important, however, is to consider how the whole matter of this education for leisure can find its roots in the young child, first in the Nursery and Infant Schools, and later in the Primary Schools. In the former group we have already noticed the value which Plato attributes to imitation and mimicry, whereas in the latter individual interests will become more obvious and independent. It is here, though with much smaller classes than today, of course, that the idea of education for leisure can be planted in the very awakening of the young child to the 'number of wonderful things' around him. From a country walk or ramble, for example, with an observant teacher, the child may derive an interest in nature-study of various kinds, ornithology, entomology, botany, and possibly even a taste for theology if the terrain warrants it. For the 'collecting instinct' is as strong nowadays as ever it was, whether it concerns badges of various kinds, or train numbers, or postage stamps. In this way hobbies can be started which may be of interest to him for the rest of his life. The Ministry of Education *Handbook of Suggestions* emphasizes this point clearly enough in the following paragraph:

> A characteristic of children during this [Primary] period which may be utilised by teachers in promoting social as well as intellectual development is the tendency to collect things . . . Teachers should see that there are suitable opportunities for the expression of this tendency.

Arrived at the Secondary school many children are seen to be reluctant to participate in such a cultural activity as mime, for example. The reason often given is that at this age they are too self-conscious to 'give themselves away', but the real reason probably is that they have never done it before. And the same holds good for other activities like music and drama. All of which goes to show that education for leisure is not an activity which can be 'picked up' at any stage in life but one which should have its roots in early childhood.

Discipline

As a postscript to this Aristotle stresses discipline as an important instrument of education, and the point has already been discussed (Chapter 2). But the question Is he right? remains to be asked; or have we been too ready to discard this instrument? There can be no one answer to this question except the fact that it is a self-imposed discipline, rather than one imposed from without, that we seek to develop in our pupils; but, where this has failed, as it frequently does, a penal discipline is introduced to redress the balance.

2 B

In dealing with the details of the curriculum and the carrying of them into practical effect, Aristotle considers the three principal instruments to be:

(*a*) intellectual, moral, and physical habits, the last-named chronologically coming first; and (*b*) teaching.

He conceives of no other instruments, however. But today we must add: the common life of the school – often an education in itself; contacts with extra-mural activities and interests; and such instruments as the school library, drama, concerts, school societies, travel, films, radio, television, programmed learning, language laboratories, and the Press.

It is not easy to see how some of these constituent parts of education would fit, if at all, into Aristotle's picture of it. Much is being done today to foster the right physical habits; for, as we have indicated, the modern view and presentation of physical education is far beyond anything that he ever dreamed of. As against his plan for keeping the body and the mind distinct, and his 'sandwich' plan for their training, we now know that there is no question of which comes first, and that physical habits depend to some extent on intellectual habits, and *vice versa*. His basic subjects, as we have seen, are not far off our three R's – though we need additions, of course. Moreover, he approves them partly for their practical uses in essential elementary skills, and partly for their value in training and discriminatory judgement, as in music and drawing. We need them for the same purpose, and the training of the discriminatory judgement in the field of the arts is particularly important in an age which is bombarded with material of all kinds from television, radio, and the Press. In addition to the basic subjects, others will be needed for direct or indirect vocational purposes.

Music in Education

While we may reject part of what he says about music as an instrument of education, for example, his restriction of the choice of instruments, and his reasons for the restrictions, we may accept the main principles underlying what he says, and, applying them in a wider field to include drama and other arts, consider current educational practice in the light of them. Thus:

(i) Performance is a necessary part of any musical or artistic training, even if it be a limited part for many older pupils. Upon it must depend both discrimination and appreciation – that is, 'appreciation' in its original sense of assessing the *value* (*pretium*) of something – and not merely liking it.

Nowadays, of course, through the wide dissemination of music through various mechanical channels one hears of very young children, aged three or even under, who can sit spellbound listening to a long-playing record of a symphony, and demanding more; but is this not simply a case of 'liking' it – for its rhythm or orchestral 'colour'? If only one could know exactly how much in quality or quantity, of such a work the infant actually does hear! Do the harmonies, for example, sound the same as they do to the ear of the musical adult? Will acoustic science ever be able to reveal this to us? If so, many of our problems in relation to the choice and use of music for the very young would be solved, and we should all be better equipped for the task of teaching. It has been found, by experience, that young children can pick up a melody more readily by listening to it sung, without accompaniment of any kind, by the parent or teacher, and that the addition of a pianoforte accompaniment only adds confusion to the young singer. Indeed, the whole effect of this addition on the mind of the child has been described by an expert as 'one big, buzzing, booming confusion'. We do know, however, that there is no essential correlation between the appreciation of rhythm and that of pitch; one and the same child may be endowed with a keen sense of rhythm, but yet have little or no sense of pitch, and *vice versa.*

The former we can usually detect by rhythmic response through bodily movement, but we cannot as yet discern *what* the tone-deaf child actually hears when a musical note is sung or played. Much less do we know what any young child hears in the way of chords or harmony; and, until we do, we are groping in the dark.

(ii) But this performance should, in general, be that of the amateur and not of the professional. School plays and school concerts, though admirable in themselves, may tend to become professionalized, and so not only occupy an inordinate amount of time but also make excessive demands on the comparatively few who participate in them. This is not, by any means, to decry first class performances, but it may be as well to remind ourselves that the play or the music is 'the thing'; for sometimes well nigh impossible standards are set. Again, should competitive festivals of music or drama be encouraged for schools? The competitive festival movement has undoubtedly done much to propagate the use of the best music, and its adjudicators have given much valuable help and advice to individual teachers, but it is only the fringe of the school population which is touched by these means, and, in each case, only the most musical. In 1927, however, a new type of festival came into being, which abolished the competitive element and threw open its doors to whole classes rather than to individual choirs, and, in so doing, stressed the corporate nature of participating in a festival. This type of festival has grown in popularity with both teachers and children down the years, and now is established all over the country. This would have also been Aristotle's ideal, no doubt.

(iii) The intellectual aspect of musical and artistic training must always be kept in view, and such training at best should always be a training of the mind. In this connexion, one has often observed an association of musical and mathematical or scientific ability in one and the same person, though the significance of it is not easy to determine. Is it because one is in complete contrast to the other, the pursuit of music offering some emotional relief, at least, to the intellectual demands of a science? Or does some acoustic element in the science or in mathematics bewitch the scientist to derive pleasure from the musical sounds he listens to? For, after all, *akouein* does mean *to listen*, and is the root from which the science of acoustics is sprung.

But whatever the real significance is, the fact remains that in so many of the smaller grammar schools in the country, where there is said to be not enough work for a full-time musician, the music teaching is, as often as not, entrusted to the science master or mistress!

(iv) And so education in music for every boy and girl should always be included as an instrument of teaching, and as part of the 'freeman's culture'. Moreover, it should prove both a stimulus and a contribution to the wise use of leisure time. Indeed, it is rightly regarded as one of the most potent factors in education for leisure, and it will be the more effective for this purpose, the more stress that is laid on enjoyment and *creative* activity as the principal aims.

2 C

This is the only place where Aristotle approaches the matter of teacher-training, but what he does say clearly implies a course both of theory and practice; elsewhere, as has been noted, he suggests a similar course for parents, to which reference has already been made on p. 31.

Under the Athenian system all teachers received more or less the same training. But in England and Wales, until after the Second World War there were, broadly speaking, two types of training, namely that for university graduates who were destined to be specialist subject teachers in Grammar and Public Schools and that for non-graduate young women, and young men, most of whom would teach a wide range of subjects in primary schools or in the non-selective secondary schools then known as Senior Schools and sometimes as secondary modern schools. But the advent of the various types of comprehensive secondary schools has changed this, and many of the most enterprising graduates desire to teach in such schools in response to the challenge to make their subject meaningful and enjoyable to boys and girls who, at least initially, are not academically-minded, often for reasons associated with their home background.

In addition, many women graduates who are married, and whose youngest child is now attending school, are taking up part-time teaching (every morning, or every afternoon) in primary schools, where their experience in bringing up their own children is at a premium. Such developments, and the courses leading to advanced teaching qualifications which are provided by University Institutes of Education, are making the teaching profession more of a unity.

But the greatest advances in the field of pedagogical study stem from: (*a*) the recognition (very belatedly in the United Kingdom) of the need for objective research in education, so that mere opinion or expediency, or financial restrictions, which have hitherto been the deciding factors of educational change, shall no longer decide issues of vital importance to the future of the nation; and (*b*) the creation of the new university degree, the Bachelor of Education, open to suitable students in the colleges of education who are prepared to study for a further year after attaining the status of qualified teacher.

The passage of the Robbins Report (1963) which led to this second development runs as follows:

> The solution that we recommend is one which . . . is very much in line with proposals in the McNair Report of nearly twenty years ago, and is a logical next step from the Institutes of Education that were set up following it. The McNair Report offered two alternative schemes for closer association between the colleges and the universities [Appendix four, Part 1, Sec. 4]. The varying arrangements made by the universities did not follow either of these precisely. What they did, however, was to bring the colleges of the region together with each other and with the University Department of Education in a federation under a University Institute of Education. They stopped a little short of the McNair Report's conception of such federations as Schools of Education of a university. We recommend a return to this basic conception, with some further features that seem to us called for by the new stage on

which the colleges are entering. . . . We also recommend that the colleges should be known in future as Colleges of Education.

On the academic side the Schools of Education should take over the functions of the present Institutes. The degrees granted to students in Colleges of Education would be degrees of the university, and in all arrangements that it made for them the School of Education would be responsible to the university senate. For this purpose the School of Education would have its own academic board as the Institutes do now for the certificate, and they would be responsible to the university for both degree and certificate work. Under the academic board would be appropriate board of studies for different subjects (as there are now such bodies under varying names, for the certificate).

No doubt, as with the proposals in the McNair Report, the universities will need time to consider what they feel able to do . . . but we would emphasise that our proposals form a whole, even though agreement on some parts of them may be possible more speedily than on others. For example, in the conditions that are certain to prevail in the mid-1960's, it will be desirable to make degrees available as quickly as possible. We must make it clear, however, that in our view, which is supported by much evidence, the current discontent in the Training Colleges is not just a matter of wanting degrees. It goes much deeper and involves the whole standing of the colleges in the system of higher education in this country.

To the solution of this problem we believe the key is an appropriate closer connection with the universities without the loss of the essential links with the local authorities and schools. . . . But clearly the scheme would fail if a substantial number of universities were unwilling to accept the responsibilities we propose. . . . They have in the past shown themselves very ready to respond to a national need, and we believe this to be one [3].

All the great advances which have taken place as a result of this strong and clear recommendation have ushered in a period of intense pedagogical thinking. Gone for ever is the time when the work of the teacher could be regarded as the instilling of information. Gone is the time when 'chalk and talk' could be regarded as the sole teaching method to be applied. Gone is the time when the publicly provided L.E.A. secondary school, unlike the independent Public Schools, could concentrate on examination results and seek to be judged by them alone, and not also by their effects on the shaping of character. We *know* now, thanks to psychological and psychiatric research, what religious people and most other thoughtful people have long believed, that the home background, and in particular the handling of the infant in the first three years of life, lays the inescapable foundation of character and outlook. But we also know that the primary school, largely through its influence on the parents, and the secondary school, by its direct action upon the adolescent in the stage which Rousseau described as 'being born again', can have profound effect in shaping and guiding human lives. We *know* now, what people used to suspect and some boldly used to declare, that the very nature of a community, its ideals, its efficiency, its outlook, and of course, its future, is very largely in the hands of the school-teachers.

But this was a view which Aristotle, like his master Plato before him, took for granted and made fundamental to all his thinking upon education.

Of course, all this lays upon the teacher a heavy responsibility. But let the teacher of today take comfort from his Athenian counterpart, who was said to enjoy his leisure (*echein scholēn*); but, curiously enough, the same Greek phrase also means to 'keep a school'; and the two meanings seem quite incompatible – until the Greek use of the operative word is understood. For *scholē* does mean 'leisure', but it also means 'that in which leisure is employed, such as a learned discussion or lecture'; and so it comes to mean the *place* where such lectures or lessons are given, that is, the school. None the less the phrase does suggest that the Athenian teacher did enjoy his work.

6 · Aristotle on Music in Education

I: THE NATURE OF GREEK MUSIC

In *Pol.* VIII, 4, 5, 6, and 7, Aristotle's views on music in education were briefly summarized and criticized; but he devoted, comparatively, so much space to the subject that these thoughts seem to require a chapter to themselves. Moreover, unless one possesses at least an elementary knowledge of what Greek music was like, it would not be easy to estimate the applicability of these views to education in music today. Why, for example, is the 'Dorian Mode' conducive to 'a moderate and settled temper', as Aristotle declares? Or what is meant by 'Harmony', when we know that Greek classical music was almost entirely unisonal, and devoid of 'harmony' in our sense of the word?

The late Professor Macran [1] wrote of a lecture on 'Music of the Past' given by a distinguished Professor of Music which included one of the few extant specimens of ancient Greek music available – a 'Hymn to Apollo'. It was, he said, unanimously regarded by all the musicians present as 'standing quite alone in its utter lack of meaning and its unredeemed ugliness'; and considerable surprise was expressed that a nation, which had amazed all succeeding generations by its excellence in the other arts, should have failed so entirely in the art *which it prized and practised most.*

In the light of subsequent knowledge, however, we now know that such a criticism is absurd; for the beauty of anything *for us* is conditioned by our power to appreciate it, which presupposes, of course, our familiarity with it or with things like it. In any case, the history of Greek music is bedevilled by confusions both ancient and modern. But it is possible to extract certain basic principles of its technique without entering into a discussion of its later and more complicated developments.

The framework of their melodies was based on the musical interval of a fourth, named a *tetrachord* (literally, four strings of the lyre) of which the higher note was the keynote or tonic. To this a second tetrachord (i.e. four more notes) was later added to complete the scale or mode, and, as music developed, further tetrachords were added. It was this joining together of tetrachords which was named 'Harmony' (*harmozein*=to join together). Hence the word was used as an alternative to the word 'mode' or scale. The intermediate notes of the tetrachord, with a prescribed minimum of two, were regarded as 'passing notes', and could fall under either of three classes:

(i) Diatonic – the simplest – employing mainly whole tones – the white notes of our pianoforte, for the most part.

(ii) Chromatic – more elaborate – using semitones as well as whole tones, i.e. the black notes as well.

(iii) Enharmonic – very complex – including quarter tones – to modern ears imaginary sounds between the black and white notes, 'between the cracks', as they might be described, or actual sounds as produced by a string instrument.

Superimposed on these, as it were, were the seven modes or scales, each starting on a different note of the mode. Thus the succession of intervals was different in each case, and the position of the keynote or tonic varied accordingly – a very important point, because in Greek music the melody always tended to circulate round it. It was thus the *order* of the tones, semitones and quarter tones which decided the class and mode to which a particular melody belonged. All this sounds somewhat complicated, and so it is, but certain relevant points about it must be taken into consideration.

(*a*) To start with, the study of Greek music is further complicated by the fact that the word *mousikē* embraced many of the other arts as well; in fact, it could be used as the equivalent of what modern civilization now terms 'culture'. Again, although there is a definite treatise on it, in our sense of the word 'music', by Aristoxenus, a pupil of Aristotle, it is not always clear to which of the arts *mousikē* refers.

(*b*) Limiting the sense of the word *mousikē* to music as *we* understand it, meant for the Greeks limiting it essentially to Song. *Melos* implies not merely melody in our restricted use of the word but also song, or poetry spoken to music; in the latter case the rise and fall of the 'melody' corresponded to the rise and fall of the spoken word, represented by the accents. Moreover, if music was primarily song for the Greeks, it was also inseparably linked with the dance; and this is shown by the frequent use of the same terms for each. *Arsis*, for example, in dance refers to the raising of the foot, and in music and poetry to the rising pitch of the singer [2].

(*c*) The music, as has been observed, consisted of a single line of melody, but when 'accompanied' by the lyre, the tune was probably 'doubled' an octave above; although later some form of descant was gradually introduced (cp. the history of medieval music).

(*d*) To return to the modes. They were seven in number, and were named after the various States of Greece – Dorian, Phrygian, etc.

The important point about them was not merely the variety and refinement of their intervals but also the position of the keynote in each case, as has been previously noted. The Hypodorian* has the lowest keynote, followed by the Hypophrygian, Hypolydian, Dorian, Phrygian, Lydian, and Mixolydian, the keynote of each mode rising a tone or semitone above its predecessor. Thus the Mixolydian is a 'high' mode because any melody composed in it must obviously lie for the most part in the upper region of the mode. A Hypodorian melody, on the same analogy, is consequently centred around the lower region of the mode.

(*e*) At the risk of falling into vain repetition, it must be emphasized that to the classical Greeks music was like a second language capable of expressing all that could be expressed in words spoken or sung. Music, in fact, conveyed to the performer or listener the mood of the words and was inseparable from it. Such an integration of speech, or song, and music is quite without parallel in modern times. Purely instrumental music was thought not to be able to effect this because, unaided by words, it could not express the ideas portrayed in the songs. In the *Laws* Plato complains of the current separation of music and poetry, which was becoming the fashion in his day. 'Music,' he wrote, 'is expressive of feeling, which may vary from calm sentiment to passionate anger, but feeling must have some substance, and this can be conveyed only by language' [2].

(*f*) Although ancient Greek poets, philosophers, and historians have written so enthusiastically about the high artistic quality of their music, nearly all written traces of it have disappeared. One of the earliest examples (408 B.C.) is a brief fragment of a chorus from the *Orestes* of Euripides on papyrus, where the musical notation (consisting of letters) is even harder to decipher than the words. The only piece of music which is preserved intact, chiselled in stone, is the *Epitaph of Seikelos* for his wife, both of which have been recorded (H.M.V. Vol. I, side 15 – *History of Music in Sound*).

(*g*) Of all the Greek writers who dealt with music Aristotle is probably the most practical and instructive. In the *Politics* he discusses music

* Hypodorian (under Dorian) means that the keynote is a fourth below that of the Dorian.

in its relation to the *State* and to morality. Here he explores more deeply than Plato did the basis of the power which it wields over thought and feeling. Moreover, Aristotle was concerned not only with the musical education of the young – to be dealt with later – but with influencing the ideas and opinions of the ordinary Athenian citizen of his day. Many of these suggestions were not put into practice until after his death.

Musical forms, Aristotle asserts, provide a true copy of the forms of moral states, and this is the basis of the various moral influences exerted by the modes. In passing, it is interesting to note the English parallelism between 'mood' and 'mode' (*tropos* for both). By some of these modes, notably by the Mixolydian (see p. 82) we are said by Aristotle to be moved to a querulous and disagreeable mood. By others such as the Hypodorian – a low, relaxed mode – we become prone to self-indulgence. On the other hand, the Dorian mode, with its keynote in the middle, was considered to be the only one which induced courage and steadfastness in the listener, while the Phrygian excited him too violently.

II: THE FUNCTION OF MUSIC IN EDUCATION

It is clear from Aristotle's statement in the *Politics* (VIII, 3) that music was an old established branch of education, a preparation for one of the proper uses of leisure, and this not as mere amusement, i.e. relying on others to provide it. At first he seems to incline to this somewhat limited view, but later extends to three the grounds on which it should be included in the curriculum. These are, he says:

(i) amusement and relaxation;

(ii) moral virtue;

(iii) the enjoyment of leisure, involving the cultivation of the *mind*.

With regard to the first, he is clear that 'youth is not to be *instructed* in music with a view to their amusement, for learning is no pleasure, but is accompanied with pain'. Does Aristotle here imply that in Athens, at any rate, the work of the school was so austere that amusements had to be taught to the accompaniment of pain? The answer would depend upon the nature of the 'amusement' which the writer had in mind. Subsequently, however, he makes a concession: 'perhaps boys may learn music for the sake of amusement, which they will enjoy when they are grown up'; 'but', he adds, 'why should they learn music themselves, and not, like the Persian kings, enjoy the pleasure and instruction derived from hearing others. For the Spartans, without learning music at all, can, as they say, judge of good and bad music?' There is certainly a simple answer to this, that most Englishmen who have not cultivated the art of music 'know what they like', i.e. like what they know, and have no taste for anything else! But the idea that boys should learn music for the sake of amusement in after-school life is probably one of general acceptance today. If, on the other hand, they merely *listened* to music, like the Persian kings, and did not make it for themselves, their capacity for intelligent musical appreciation would surely be considerably limited. For, in the modern sense, musical experience is of two kinds, active and passive. We make music ourselves, and listen to others making it. Vital art must be creative, whether by singing in a choir or playing in an orchestra, or actually composing music; and anyone who is content *merely* to listen stands only on the threshold of the art.

Another reason for learning music, Aristotle reminds us, is its introduction into social gatherings and entertainments, 'because it makes the hearts of men glad, and provides relaxation'. To this idea most teachers would whole-heartedly subscribe, for is there any other art which can so draw children together in the enjoyment of one common purpose?

Finally, the question whether children should themselves be taught to sing or play is settled after much deliberation. Aristotle now concedes that 'it is difficult, if not impossible, for those who do not perform to be good judges of music'. Then follows a penetrating sentence or two, the implications of which we have been slow to recognize – even in the twentieth century. 'Children should have *something to do*, and the rattle of Archytas, which people give to their children in order to amuse them and prevent them breaking anything in the house, was a capital invention, for a young thing cannot be quiet. The rattle is a toy suited to the infant mind, and musical education is a rattle or toy for children of larger growth.'

It was not so very long ago that Jacques Dalcroze, harnessing this natural activity and restlessness of young children to the rhythms of music, explored some of the possibilities of Eurhythmics – apparently very much on ancient Greek lines, for is not the very name of it a Greek word?

The 'rattle', too, both for infants and older children, would seem to be the prototype of the modern percussion band as well as the instrumental 'battery' of Carl Orff.

Granted that children should learn music for amusement, as well as for gaining some standard of appreciation in later life, 'is it degrading or vulgarizing, as some assert?' Aristotle answers that it is all a matter of degree, which can only be determined by observance of the 'happy mean', and this, in the last resort, is determined by the legislator. In any case, 'the pupil should stop short of the arts which are practised in professional contests, and do not seek to acquire those fantastic wonders of execution which have passed into education'. Moreover, the learning of music ought not to impede the business of riper years. In fact, the pupil should always maintain his 'amateur status'; none the less, he adds, 'let the young pursue their studies until they are able to feel delight in noble melodies and rhythms'. With this peculiar Greek notion of the inferiority of the professional 'who plies for hire' compared with the amateur who makes music for the love of it, the Courts of Europe, during the eighteenth century, were much in sympathy. Their princes and dukes engaged famous musicians, Haydn and Mozart for example, to entertain their guests, but kept them for the most part 'below stairs'. Times indeed have changed, but in England, at any rate, it has taken many centuries to give the professional musician his merited status in society.

The effects of music on character

So much for the approval of music culture in principle. 'Music is pursued, not only as an alleviation of past toil but also as providing recreation.' 'But,' says Aristotle, 'may it not have also some influence over the character and the soul? It *must* have such an influence if characters *are* affected by it. Besides, when they hear dramatic representations, even unaccompanied by music, their feelings move in sympathy. On the other hand, there is a representation of character in songs, for the musical modes differ essentially from one another, and those who hear them are affected differently by each. Some of them make us sad and grave like the Mixolydian' (where the keynote lies low in the mode).

'Others, again, produce a moderate and settled temper like the Dorian, while the Phrygian inspires. And the same holds good about the rhythms also, for some have a more stable, and others a more energetic, character; and of the latter, some are more vulgar in their emotional effect, and others more liberal.'

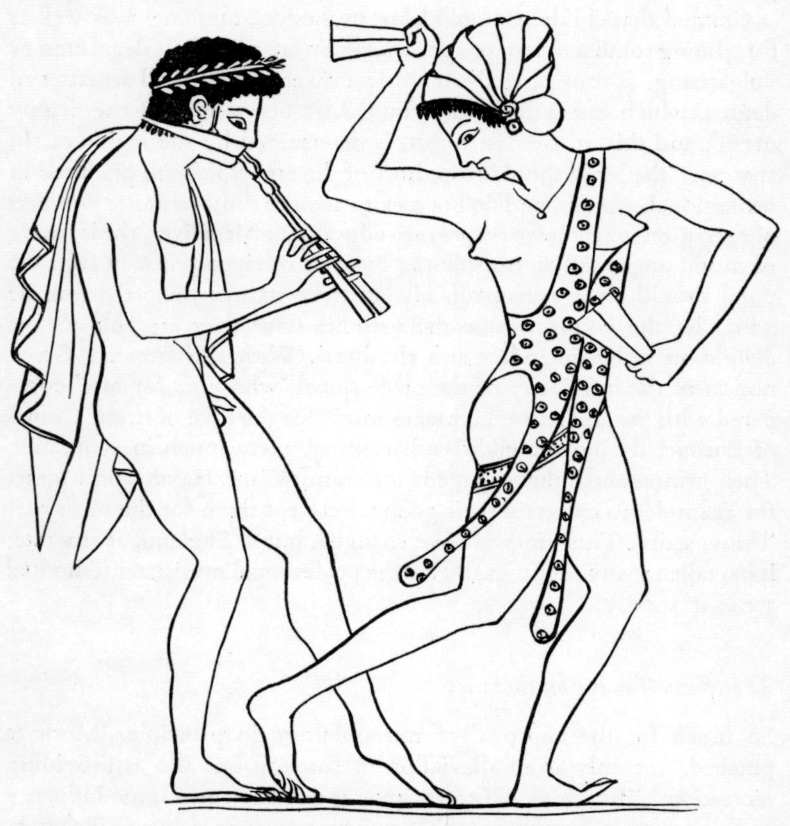

FIG I The *aulos*, played to accompany dancing

From these principles Aristotle proceeds to discuss what instruments should be used in musical education. Not pipes (*auloi*), nor any other 'professional instrument' such as the harp, but 'such as will make the pupils attentive, either at their musical training, or in other lessons'. The pipe was out of favour because it was associated with the worship of Bacchus, and because, 'when played, it prevents the use of speech'.

Moreover, according to Professor Geiringer, it has a shrill and strident tone, more like an oboe than a flute, as it has often been mistranslated by the inexpert. For it was fitted with a double reed, was made in

FIG 2 The *aulos* and the lyre, played by two muses. The sitting muse produces notes to enable the standing muse to tune her instrument

several sizes, and was usually played in pairs. It was not held between the performer's lips, like our modern oboes are, but was inserted bodily in the mouth. Perhaps that was why Athene threw her *aulos* away in disgust, because it disfigured her mouth!

It is not surprising, therefore, that this instrument, because of its high efficiency, sufficed for the musical accompaniments of the Greek drama. It is not known for certain why it was played in pairs, as in the illustration. In earlier times the accompanying *aulos* may have sustained a 'drone' – as in the Scottish bag-pipe – while, in later times, the notes of the accompaniment may have been more frequently varied. The *kithara*, seen in the illustration, is simply a larger form of lyre [3].

FIG 3 A flying *nike* holding a *kithara*. The instrument is played with a plectrum inserted between the strings

Other instruments, too, were rejected because of the skill required to play them competently; and the only other instrument Aristotle does not mention by name in this connexion was the lyre, the instrument of the *dilettante* and the novice, which was to the Athenian what the pianoforte was to the English middle-class of the last century. So this, presumably, was the most popular instrument in schools.

Aristotle summarizes the discussion by saying that the young must be directed to music and trained in it, provided always that 'the most excellent rhythms and melodies are used'.

FIG 4 The lyre, played with a plectrum

But did all this really result in what has been referred to as 'the moral genius' of the Greeks? It is a matter of historical fact that neither Plato nor Aristotle, by their writings, had much influence on contemporary educational practice. It must be remembered, however, that these two philosophers knew Athens only when her best days were over, and when the vigorous and intelligent population of its Golden Age had been emaciated by war and pestilence.

Plato's brief story, in the *Laws*, of the musical revolution in Athens, written about the mid-fourth century B.C. is worth summarizing.

> Our music was once divided into its proper forms. Prayers were one form of ode, named 'hymns', opposed to which were dirges, paeans [hymns to Apollo] and dithyrambs [poems of a lofty but bombastic style]. It was not permitted to change the melodic style of these established forms. There were no whistles, unmusical mob noises, or clapping for applause. The rule was to listen silently and learn; boys, teachers, and the crowd were kept in order by threat of the stick.
>
> But later an unmusical anarchy was led by poets who had natural talent, but were ignorant of the laws of music. Over-intoxicated with love of pleasure and wine, they deceived themselves into thinking that there was no right or wrong standard in music; that it was to be judged for the pleasure it gave. By their works and theories they infected the masses to think they were adequate judges [2].

None the less, the moral teaching, largely through 'Music' – in their comprehensive meaning of the term – which the majority of the population had received over the years, helped to influence, in no small measure, the Stoic ideal of moral virtue, to hand on to the Roman Empire a philosophy of life, and to Christianity a basis for ethics. Nor did this education produce a nation of sallow-faced aesthetes, for Xenophon in his *Memorabilia* certainly corrects any mistaken views we may hold on their 'aestheticism'.

> In international singing contests no-one could surpass the Athenians, yet it is not only in the beauty of voice, or in stature, or strength that they are superior to others, but in the ambition that fires them to noble and honourable achievement.

What, then, is the relevance of all this to modern education?

First and foremost, the most striking point about the whole discussion is the considerable attention given to music in Book 8 of the *Politics*. This was primarily because the legislators saw in it a good moral influence on children in general. It is significant that, in the beginnings of mass education in England in the last century, music was employed to convey moral ideals through the words of the songs. The learning of music, that is to say, was inseparably bound up with religious and moral training; but is it so today? We have our songs, ribald and sex-ridden at one end of the scale, and at the other we have noble and soul-stirring melodies. Have all these any moral influence, one way or another, on our youth of today, or are they impervious to the implications of the words? We simply do not know, and we dare not generalize; but it does seem a fair assumption that these various types of song may have some such influence, as Aristotle contended. After all, the origin of the impulse to make music is primarily to express emotion, and the Athenians, as has been observed, prescribed such music and songs as were regarded as expressing desirable emotions; and it was the habitual practice of such music which, by association with a certain mood, apparently caused the boys to wish for no other. Aristotle, however, also makes mention of a possible 'loop-hole' – in listening to 'music of a passionate and energetic character' when others, i.e. professional musicians, are performing. These are not to be employed in education, of course, but are suitable for relaxation and amusement. Dare we assume that the schoolboys of Athens delighted in this performance of 'pop' music as a pleasant relief from the rigour of the Dorian and other like melodies which they sang in school?

But the supreme legacy of this Athenian musical education, as far as it concerns us, is the considerable importance they attached to the education and training of the emotions of the young. Let it be remembered, in passing, that Sparta scorned music – with the result that the Spartans, although renowned in war, were not to be compared with the Athenians in enlightenment and artistic predominance.

> As to the power of music over the emotions, there can be no difference of opinion. Nobody who can distinguish one tune from another can doubt the emotional effect of music, and, on the whole, the very largely ennobling effect upon the emotions.
>
> There is a passage in *Boswell's Life of Johnson* where the author declares that when he hears music he wishes to get up and fight for his country. To which the Sage replies, 'Sir, if music made me feel such a fool, I should never listen to it.' But Johnson is speaking of an excess and a degradation of the right thing; it is certainly not degrading nor footling to feel moved on hearing the 'Marseillaise' or the Finale of Beethoven's Ninth Symphony. Yet in English schools we have to a large extent neglected this important side of education. Although music, as we know, actually concerns the whole man – physical, emotional and intellectual, education is too often limited to schemes of work devised for the passing of examinations, while the consideration of music and the other arts is still largely disregarded, even in 'high places' [4].

Is this part of the answer to so much of the unbridled sexual licence which prevails today? John Curwen, that pioneer of music teaching in the last century, once wrote:

> The ordinary school text book may well cultivate the reasoning and the memory, but it seldom does anything for the imagination or the emotions. It is vitally important for us that our children should *feel* rightly as well as *think* correctly, that they should *love* truly as well as *reason* deeply.

Happily, however, music therapy is slowly finding its way into hospitals and other institutions for the care of mentally and physically disabled children. Nervous disorders, too, in children are being dispelled in many cases by the rhythm and orderliness with which music is so largely concerned; and does not this curative principle derive from that of Aristotle, who pointed the way in his doctrine of the cathartic or purifying effects of music on distressed minds (*Politics* VIII)? We may well ask at this stage. Could some of these mental disorders have been *prevented* by giving music and the arts 'fair play' in our educational system?

In point of fact, music does not get fair play in our present educational system, not, at any rate, as far as some of our L.E.A.s are concerned. On the other hand, the Ministry of Education (to use its more familiar title, perhaps) in its handbooks of suggestions to teachers has time and again stressed the value of music both in the corporate and aesthetic life of the school, not to mention its importance in the disciplined use of leisure. But the estimate of this value unfortunately varies from one L.E.A. to another. In some areas, for example, there are official musical advisers whose work of visiting the school, and giving helpful advice is a great boon to the music teachers in them. In others there is no such provision made, and those who teach music in their schools have to rely on their own – often very limited – experience. By comparison Physical Education fares far better, for there can scarcely be left in the country one L.E.A. which does not employ at least two P.E. advisers – one for boys, and one for girls.

Again, in some areas, the L.E.A. provides facilities for pupils in their schools to learn various musical instruments on the school premises, if they so desire it. Considerable as has been the steady growth of instrumental music in some L.E.A. schools in recent years, it is by no means the case that all of them give equal, or even adequate, facilities for it, indeed, such provision is still the exception rather than the rule.

Moreover, it is only quite recently that, as a result of unremitting demands, special rooms for music teaching and music-making have been 'allowed', whereas in far too many schools in the country music has to be taught when and where there is available space and place for it.

Further, after long experience in conducting massed choirs of pupils from L.E.A. schools in many parts of the country, one is struck by the considerable preponderance of girls over boys on these occasions. Does this imply that girls are more 'musical' than boys? Far from it; but this outmoded, Victorian, idea is very slow in dying. The truth is that our boys' schools, both Grammar and Secondary Modern, are very short of competent, well-trained, music *masters*. And this is not to be wondered at when one knows that in far too many boys' and mixed Grammar schools, the boys' music classes cease after Form 2, because their voices are said to be 'breaking' (though they are really only, in the course of nature, *changing*), in spite of all evidence to the contrary from the touch-line on the football field! Whatever the reason, the fact remains that the majority of these boys, thus losing contact with music-making, also lose interest in it. Therefore, when some of them later are admitted to a College of Education, it is no wonder that so few of them are ready or willing to take a course in music. With these considerations in mind, it is not difficult to see that music does not as yet receive fair play in our educational system; it has not yet attained *in practice* the status of the other subjects on the timetable. Indeed, it is often referred to as its 'Cinderella'. But if it be remembered that, after all, Cinderella did go to the Ball, and marry the Prince, there is still hope for her!

Finally, Aristotle hints at a musical education for the intellect, but stops short at any development of the idea. Such an education would possibly have included acoustics in relation to musical instruments, the history of music beginning with Homer, as well as a survey of the other arts, drama, poetry, and dancing, so closely connected with music.

In these days the study of 'Advanced Music' is largely confined to the universities and colleges of music but, to judge from the infinitesimal proportion of candidates who offer 'A' level music in the various G.C.E. examinations, it receives but scant attention in our schools.

One of the reasons for this may be the old and die-hard idea that while music appeals to the emotions, literature concerns mainly the intellect; it is time to make a strong protest, for both appeal to both. Music is just as much

> a language as English, with a notation, a grammar and literature of its own. Every great melody has got a meaning, like the great lines of Shakespeare, or of Milton, or of Virgil, as full of meaning and significance for those who study them. There is a similar parallel between music and drama; when one considers the texture of the dialogue of some of the greatest plays ever written, it is not difficult to see that the design of a Mozart *Quintet* or a Beethoven *Trio* is just as complete as the dialogue of any great dramatist. Again, all the great masterpieces of music are built on as intelligible a plan as the plot of a great play. Thus music contains all the delights of the study of a language, of a great literature, as well as the same kind of analytical problems to be met with in the study of a science [4].

Would Aristotle have commended this to some of his 'leisured sages' had he been living today? Add to all this the musical terms which the music of the Greeks has handed down to us: the orchestra, where the Chorus danced and the musicians now play, symphony, harmony, polyphony, as well as the word music itself. The foundation of operatic style in Europe was based upon the principles of Greek drama during the seventh century B.C. – yet another aspect of their genius and its meaning for us. All this, and a great deal more besides, is summed up in the words of Marion Bauer in *A Narrative History of Music*.

> In Greece, for the first time, music had obtained the dignity of any Art, with all its aesthetic, emotional, and moral significance, with its complicated theory, its sophisticated technique, consciously employed to give pleasure, and to uplift the spirit of man [5].

But there is one fundamental attitude to the study of music teaching on which we must part company with both Aristotle and Plato. It will be remembered that both insisted on the importance of retaining the use of certain modes and melodies because of their proved beneficial effect on the characters. However excellent the motive, they evidently did not foresee that music, even the comparatively simple music of their day, could and would develop – and that, without detriment to the morals of the young. In this matter, therefore, they must be regarded as counter-revolutionaries.

It remains for us to ask whether *our* teachers of music in Colleges and Schools are any better in this respect – which, in the opinion of one out-spoken critic at least, they certainly are not.

> Nothing short of a revolution is needed in school music. Action seems to be limited to introducing mild, very dated jazz, or rather, some of its clichés, without any of its essence.
>
> Since the beginning of the century, musical educators have been stubborn and insistent upon basing all training on music of the past. . . . Meanwhile things go from bad to worse: the rate of change in style is such that there is more difference between the music of 1900 and 1960 than between that of 1500 and 1900 – and still the presses continue to turn out music in outmoded styles, adding further both to the door barring the way of the young to music of today. . . . Is it therefore surprising that the younger generation regards classical music as music of the past, and 'pop' music as music of the present? What alternative does the teacher offer? Why is he irate at his pupils' interest in 'pop'? Surely he should be worried about those who are *un*interested in 'pop', the only music of today they hear.

Rightly, he compares modern progress in science, art (and he might add many other 'subjects') during the past sixty years with the *status quo* in music teaching [6].

To many this may sound an exaggerated story written by a revolutionary, but, in general, it is substantially true. Of course, there are a few pioneers courageously blazing new trails, but the rank and file of teachers can scarcely be said to be following them. Have we, in fact, earned a reputation in music teaching best described by a slight emendation to the old latin tag *Tempora mutantur, et non* (not *nos*) *mutamur in illis*?

7 · Education for Leisure

Within thirty years there will probably be compulsory education for adults, according to the Dean of the Divisions of General Studies at New York University, Dr Milton R. Stern. Writing in the Divisions magazine *Pleasures in Learning* [1], he observed that by then everyone will have more leisure than he knows what to do with on account of automation and the like, and what someone learns in his teens may well be out of date by the time he is thirty. We have agreed as a people that education is good both for society and for the individual. To this Dr Stern adds, 'So in tomorrow's house there may be a study hour for the whole family.' Aristotle, of course, saw the necessity for this many centuries ago, when he prescribed education for children and for adults as well. But how far have *we*, as a nation, progressed towards this goal? When one considers the use of leisure by the vast majority of our people at the present time – in the public house, at the cinema, gambling, bingo, *watching* various forms of sport, television 'fever', the outlook is none too promising. Lest the author be dubbed a species of puritan kill-joy, he would not dare to condemn any of these forms of entertainment when indulged in with moderation. But what is the prospect for a people whose whole idea of leisure is concentrated solely on one or other of these forms; a people whose manifold skills and talents are as yet dormant and unexpended?

And what of the Press? By far the largest circulation is achieved by those newspapers which *exploit* sex and sensationalism – let us face it. Is this *malaise* an indirect result of two World Wars? For the Victorians, despite their prudery, hypocrisy, and complacency, were, on the whole, a decent lot. Their most flagrant delinquency was the inability or refusal to 'see those things which were coming after'. And so it was that, following the First World War there was a period of devastating unemployment, when demobilized men and women could find no work to do; and so one of the many makeshifts introduced by the government (only sporadically, be it said) which was intended to keep the many unemployed school-leavers off the streets – for a time, at any rate – was the Day Continuation School, to which allusion has already been made in an earlier chapter. For these boys and girls compulsory attendance was enjoined for eight hours a week until they reached the age of fifteen, the school-leaving age being then at fourteen. The curriculum was based on the current Elementary School régime, but was, for the most part, devoid of craft-work of any kind, since the only buildings available were not equipped for it. There was, however, one such school in Bermondsey, sponsored by the Oxford and Bermondsey Clubs Council, which was in some ways different from the others. For, by an internal arrangement, it was agreed that truant members of the school should not be admitted to the clubs (which were then very popular) unless they attended the school regularly. Here, at least, was the germ of a friendly relationship between club and school. But no sooner had the experiment got under way than the whole scheme was abandoned, and the Day Continuation School came to an untimely end, except as has been previously stated a few which were retained for the use of some of the employers in various government undertakings. But none of this had the remotest connexion with education for leisure, though the Oxford and Bermondsey Clubs did touch the fringe of it with their encouragement of sports, games, and athletics in well equipped centres. By the end of the Second World War the government of the day had learnt its lesson, and the prospect of employment for the demobilized was far more hopeful. Vocational training was made available for the large majority of those who desired it, and industry was progressively supplied with workers, owing to the gradual demobilization of the armed forces.

Meanwhile many voluntary bodies, the Workers' Educational Association, for example, sought to foster an interest in various cultural pursuits among the adult workers, but again with only very limited results. And what of youth? When the vaguely termed Youth Movement (which came into being during these years) rose to the dignity of a Youth Service there were signs that the government were 'out for culture'. At any rate, the wholly inadequate grants which were given did for a time strengthen the hands of such voluntary bodies who had for years been fighting a losing battle. At least the very idea of a government-sponsored Youth Service gave them a new status. But the general effect of it scarcely outlasted the Second World War.

Now there seem to be two ways of tackling this whole problem of education for leisure at the present time, one at the school end, and the other at the adult end. As to the former, the possibility of interesting young children in various leisure-worthy pursuits has already been discussed in Chapter 2, and the larger the school the wider will be the variety of hobbies which can be introduced. But it is in the secondary schools where the test of *concentration* on one, or on a number, of special interests really comes, and it is here that the various clubs, groups, or societies within the school, whether meeting in or out of school hours, have such an important part to play in the cultivation of countless desirable pursuits. And there would appear to be a kind of two-way traffic involved here. Some of the pursuits followed in these voluntary gatherings might well react favourably on the subjects studied in class lessons. To take only one instance out of innumerable others: members of a drama group might well find their interest in English language and literature lessons considerably stimulated as a result of this popular group activity. On the other hand, some subjects taught in class might give some pupils an urge to join the corresponding group; music, art, biology, geology, astronomy, are perhaps some of the most obvious potentials in this connexion.

But to bring this to anything like fruition, even after the raising of the school-leaving age in 1970, the school day would have to be lengthened, as finally urged in the Newsom Report. The idea of the Day-Boarding School (dare we refer to it as the Day-Board School?) to which children go at breakfast time and stay until the evening, as advocated by Sir Leon Bagrit in his Reith Lectures [2], is by no means new. It has frequently been advocated as a means of providing a more adequate number of hours in which to educate *pupils* of *particular promise*. But why not for *all* pupils, wherever practical? For, to quote the lecturer's own words:

> During this much lengthened school day it should be easier to instil in them the type of attitudes which are necessary if we are going to develop the social conscience and sense of social responsibility which an age of plenty is going to demand. It would give time for some handicraft, art or music [and, we might add, many another such 'leisurely' pursuits] and for visits to theatres, and concerts, and exhibitions – which, at present, are mainly an occasional and intermittent experience. It is essential, in my opinion, that all children, especially in their teens, should be exposed to artistic, musical, and other cultural influences as widely and as frequently as possible. This is not a luxury, to be reserved for the fortunate *élite*; it is an absolute necessity.

But for a couple of decades such hobby activities after school hours, and up to 9 or 10 p.m. for the oldest pupils, have been organized in Sweden: the scheme began in Gothenburg some thirty years ago and gradually spread to other urban areas of high population density. Most of the persons who run the clubs are not teachers, though some of the women may have been teachers before marriage, but people who are such 'amateurs' of their skill (amateur in Aristotle's sense) that they are willing to give up a week for a small payment just in order to have the joy of infecting young people with their enthusiasm for instrumental music of all kinds, art of many kinds, including such things as wood and stone carving, book binding, woodwork, metalwork, needlework, cookery (for boys as well as girls) and a long and variable list of other activities. For the younger children the activities start soon after the end of afternoon school; the oldest go home to do their homework and come back at 7 or 8 p.m. So the school 'plant' for all these activities is profitably used for an extra four or five hours a day.

Whenever the 'go-ahead' is given, is there any reason why every grammar school (if still functioning as such), every secondary modern school (with the same proviso), and every comprehensive school should not become a cultural centre for a whole area – in fact, an extension of the Cambridgeshire Village College scheme all over the country, not least in the great cities?

Beginning from the other end – the adult end – there are numerous organizations, such as amateur dramatic and operatic societies, adult choirs, choral societies, and orchestras, women's institutes, and athletic clubs, scattered throughout the length and breadth of the land, many of which find continual difficulty in attracting the younger type of recruit; indeed, many of their members are well on in middle age. But how far do their members, as a whole, *go out of their way* to attract the under twenty-ones, many of whom may possess as yet undiscovered artistic or musical talent? There could be in every small town, at least, in the country a Performing Arts Council and special interest committee, such as are growing up in some of the smaller towns in America, and finding support from some of the local industrial 'magnates'. While the intensification of arts activities has not, apparently, been the only reason for their support

> it has been an important factor in convincing industrial management, who have large industrial centres, that their people will find here a balanced community which includes a growing cultural awareness. Many of those who have come to the community are now making a direct personal contribution to the new aesthetic atmosphere [3].

In many instances the local paper contributes a 'lively arts' page every week, with its community calendar of cultural events and undertakings, local concert, drama, and art reviews, together with programme notes for the various concerts and plays advertised. There is, therefore, no overlapping of important events, as so frequently happens with us, because they are carefully dated after consultation with the local Arts Council. It need scarcely be added that such communities foster the cultural interests not only of children and adolescents, but of adults as well.

What of the immediate future of our adult population, faced with the growing power of automation and mechanization? The same problem is even more acute in the United States. Dr Milton Stern writes:

> Next year, for instance, some 50,000 steel workers will, by contract, be given a thirteen-week 'sabbatical'. This is the beginning of the inexorable new trend. Soon many millions of white-collar and factory workers will have the same opportunity. Or will they regard it as such? Dan Wakefield in an article in *The Nation* (April 1963) entitled 'Labour Shudders at Leisure' points out 'The burden of leisure, long the exclusive curse of the rich, is now the darkest threat to the well-being of the working man and the subject of increasing concern on the part of organised labour. For the first time in its history, organised labour is working for a shorter week than its leaders or its members actually want' [1].

There has always been a tendency to underrate the cultural potentialities of the man in the street, whose main interests are assumed to lie in football, racing, and gambling. If this is so, our whole educational system must bear at least some of the blame, and, more especially, the Training Colleges, whose products have been responsible for the education of 75 per cent of our children for the past two or three generations of them. In point of fact there is nothing incompatible in the idea of a mill-hand being entranced by the subtle charm of Milhaud, or of a bar-tender being inspired by the sparkling rhythms of Meyerbeer! Let it be remembered that when John Curwen first introduced the simple system of Sol-fah for music reading, about the middle of the last century, thousands of 'working men' flocked to his classes, and, as a result, especially in the industrial North and in Wales, for the first time in their lives found a new artistic satisfaction in founding male voice choirs and brass bands, many of which were subsidized by their employers. But all this gallant enterprise was surely shattered by the incidence of two world wars, and so we have had to begin all over again. The instance of music is taken because it is obviously the most *communal* of all the arts, and nowadays it is for ever at our beck and call; indeed, it is always 'there' whether we want it or not.

The concept of the ordinary working man having cultural interests of the same kinds and quality as the upper-middle class is no new one. Nor is the recognition that education is the means of bringing this about a development in thought of the twentieth century.

Nearly two hundred years ago, in the inspired volume entitled *Sketch for a Historical Picture of The Progress of the Human Mind* a book completed under the shadow of death, the Marquis de Condorcet wrote:

> The degree of equality in education that we can reasonably hope to attain, but that should be adequate, is that which excludes all dependence, either forced or voluntary. We shall show how this condition can be easily attained in the present state of human knowledge even by those who can study only for a small number of years in childhood, and then during the rest of their life in their few hours of leisure. We shall prove that, by a suitable choice of syllabus and of methods of education, we can teach the citizen everything that he needs to know in order to be able to manage his household, administer his affairs and employ his labour and his faculties in freedom; to know his rights and to be able to exercise them; to be acquainted with his duties and fulfil them satisfactorily; to judge his own and other men's actions according to his own lights *and to be a stranger to none of the high and delicate feelings which honour human nature* (this author's italics); not to be in a state of blind dependence upon those to whom he must entrust his affairs or the exercise of his rights; to be in a proper condition to choose and supervise them; to be no longer the dupe of those popular errors which torment man with superstitious fears and chimerical hopes; to defend himself against prejudice by the strength of his reason alone; and, finally, to escape the deceits of charlatans who would lay snares for his fortune, his health, his freedom of thought and his conscience under the pretext of granting him health, wealth and salvation.

But the conception of a full and balanced life needs to be taught, and yet not everyone is interested in, or understands the art of music – or of painting, the joys of hobbies in ornithology, entomology, astronomy, for the matter of that. But still there must be countless people with countless potentialities in all walks of life 'who have never been *exposed* to the cultural riches available'. And now history is repeating itself; for there is evidence that the Institute of Directors have a scheme for supporting musicians, artists, and artistic ventures in addition to such facilities are already provided by many large multiple firms; just as was done by industrialists a century or more ago. And why are such schemes advocated and put into effect? Is it not because their employees will enjoy their leisure more fully and profitably – and, possibly, work better as a result? Of course, big business has no *right* to fashion the inclinations of its employees, but an increasing number of shareholders, even, are evidently beginning to realize that a well-considered use of leisure is not without its influence on the work done in the shop, office, field, or factory.

And so the idea of adult education – for those past school age – has a new significance today because of the leisure time many are getting. Indeed, at least one L.E.A. preposes to form a department of leisure to co-ordinate and develop all the artistic and sporting activities in the city, with a 'chief' in charge. It would set a pattern for the nation.

> Leisure, of course, is the Key to the civilisation of men. Philosophy, music, and art do not seem to flourish among people who work fourteen hours a day. But American life has changed. For the first time training for leisure on a wholesale scale is necessary.

And, finally:

> We should take a long look at our stereotypes of work and leisure. We face a new period in history in which the concept of work, as we have known it, will undergo changes of tremendous import. If the world survives, it will mean in 2057 something quite different from what it has meant for thousands of years. Equally, it seems clear that *leisure* – regarded now as, in effect, released time from work – will undergo refinement as a concept. As each of us starts to ponder these meanings, we may feel that sense of mastery of the environment which is the hallmark of the civilised man [1].

Such are the views propounded by one of America's most farseeing sages, as he looks to the future of his country with guarded optimism, but with no illusions as to the complexities of a problem which we all are constrained to encounter.

Epilogue

'It's all Greek to me' is a phrase frequently heard on the lips of educated men and women when they light upon something which they cannot fully understand. The same expression, reinforced by a shrug of the shoulders, might be used by some readers of this book; partly because they are not particularly interested in educational processes, and partly because they have never enjoyed the privilege of reading Greek. To such it is probably described, and not without a certain depreciatory insinuation, as a 'dead language'. But to those who, like the late Professor Richard Livingstone [1] and others, have studied the Greek genius and its meaning to us, Greek is by no means a 'dead language'. On the contrary, 'being dead, it yet speaketh'. In his searching analysis of the old Greek way of life, Livingstone found so much that is akin to *our* way of life in this twentieth century. In the realm of intellect – 'for the Greek was the only *thinking* civilization before our own' – they gave us many keys to the language of science and philosophy in such words as zoology, physiology, psychology, politics, tyranny, democracy, history, and the like, and hybrid words as well – half Greek, half Latin, of which 'television' is an obvious example.

Our debt to them in the matter of education, in many of its various branches, is great, as we have already remarked, and is still in the process of being paid. And what of Greek art, architecture, sculpture, and, above all, its literature and drama, none of which have ever been surpassed in modern Europe? Plutarch, who lived in the first century of our era (see the timetable on p. 105), after describing the artistic glories of Athens in the days of Pericles, draws this significant conclusion:

> The reason why the works of Pericles are all the more remarkable is that they were created in a short space of time *for all time*. Each of them, in its

beauty, was at one and the same time new and antique: but, in the vivacity of its vigour, it looks, even at the present time, fresh and recently wrought. Such is the flowering of perpetual freshness to be discerned in these his works, which gives them the appearance of being untarnished by age, as though the unwavering breath of a timeless spirit had inspired them [1].

And this is surely true of all these creative works of art. It is, therefore, much to be regretted that we are so seldom privileged to see and hear these products of the Golden Age of Greece – the tragedies and comedies, for example – on our television screens. No doubt the purists would demur to this owing to the necessity of translating their literature into our language, but it is not unreasonable to make a virtue of necessity in their case. As to the art of ancient Greek music, while its use in the normal curriculum of our schools could scarcely be even considered, it was ancient Greece which first realized its possibilities in disciplining the emotions.

Again, our British democratic system, indeed our whole way of life is more akin to that of the Greeks than to that of the Romans.

Our form of government does not enter into rivalry with the institutions of others. We do not copy our neighbours, but are an example to them. It is true that we are called a democracy, for the administration is in the hands of the many, and not the few. But while the Law secures equal justice to all alike in their private disputes, the claim of excellence is also recognised: and where a citizen is in any way distinguished, he is preferred to the Public Service, not as a matter of privilege, but as a reward of merit. Neither is poverty a bar, but a man may benefit his country, whatever be the obscurity of his condition. There is no exclusiveness in our public life, and in our private intercourse we are not suspicious of each other, nor angry with our neighbour if he does what he likes: we do not put on sour looks at him which, though harmless, are not pleasant.

While we are thus unconstrained in our private intercourse, a spirit of reverence pervades our public acts; we are prevented from doing wrong by respect for authority and for the laws, having a special regard for those which are ordained for the protection of the injured, as well as for those unwritten laws which bring upon the transgressor of them the reprobation of the common feeling of the people [1].

These are sentences from the Funeral Oration of Pericles, the great Athenian leader, during the war with Sparta. One passage in this memorable speech seems to enshrine the statesman's conviction of what the democratic life of Athens should be, although he must have known quite well the faults and failings of its people, as well as the great qualities of which they were capable.

THE AGE OF PERICLES 470–399 B.C.

		Philosophers
445 B.C.	Athens and Sparta conclude a thirty years' peace treaty, each recognising the dominion of the other – Sparta on land, and that of Athens by sea.	Socrates 470–399 B.C.
431 B.C.	Increasing power of Athens under Pericles, and the jealousy it aroused in Sparta led to a sudden termination of the peace treaty, and to the Peloponnesian War, which once and for all disrupted the states of Greece from end to end. During its course, first Sparta, then Thebes became the leading power in Greece.	Plato 427–347 Aristotle 384–322
365 (*circa*)	There was a temporary Athenian revival when the Aegean confederacy was formed.	
348 B.C.	The struggle with Macedon begins; first under Philip, and then under his son Alexander, who was the pupil of Aristotle for some years.	Plutarch *circa* A.D. 100

FIG. 5 Chronological table for the periods referred to in this book.

In reading the whole of the speech with careful attention to detail (we can almost picture the speaker's gestures by the help of the various significant Greek particles appended to words, suggesting some responsive movement of the hands or arms), we realize that it stresses two main points. First, that the Athenian people as a whole actually constituted the State in a more real sense than had been conceived by any other state of Greece, all taking an equal share in its government, its education, and its pleasures. Secondly, that this parity of right and advantage gave to all the citizens more liberty to develop individual talent than was possible elsewhere in Greece. Here, then, was expressed the pattern of the 'good life' which Aristotle claimed to be 'the true end of the city-state – the full and free culture of the individual aiming at the advantage of the whole community' [2].

Are not these also an honest expression of the main aims and ideals of the majority of our people in this country today? To the Greek, at any rate, *aretē* did mean 'worth' or 'virtue' (goódness). To the Roman, *virtus* meant predominantly the *worth* of bravery. To us, has a man's 'worth' come to mean merely the amount of money he possesses? Of course, it will be objected that all this was so easy in a small city-state like Athens, and, after all, Pericles, whatever the character of his private life, did live in an ideal world of his own. But, it must be repeated, that when we relate his idealism to the Britain of today we discern a picture of what *we* are trying to achieve in our 'political' life today, especially in the field of education with its many complex problems.

It will probably be objected again that the city-state was a small self-contained unit, and consequently was ever reluctant to unite with others, even in the face of a common enemy, for fear of losing its independence. But have *we* advanced very much farther on the road to a realization of an United Europe – the United States of Europe? What caused the disintegration of the League of Nations? Was it the hard core of nationalism, and the fear of losing independence? Or was it because Europe – especially the United Kingdom and France, refused to impose sanctions on Japan when she invaded Manchuria?

In the matter of religion, which in this country at any rate is being discussed more than ever it was before, the same principle of freedom in Ancient Greece prevailed. It is something of a paradox, however, that Socrates who, if Plato truly represents his master's teaching, was no lover of freedom, was condemned to death for what was considered to be an extravagant abuse of it.

Nevertheless, the Greeks were not necessarily irreligious. It was not that they had no gods; they had too many; and, since these were created in the image of men, they were 'too much the creation of their own worshippers ever to become absolute'. When the apostle Paul, while visiting Athens, saw a statue erected 'To the Unknown God' there perhaps he saw the ultimate result of polytheism; for that is what a galaxy of gods tends to become. But their real 'religion' was clearly humanism; it followed from the 'humanizing' of their gods. They believed that man – 'the measure of all things' – without divine revelation of any kind, could, by virtue of his human nature alone, and did at times, fulfil his ideals.

In recent years our nation has been described by some as pagan, by others as materialistic, and, if the depth of our religion is to be judged by the number of those who actually cultivate it (one in ten), it can only be described as somewhat shallow. Has this, by the way, any connexion with the increase in crime of various forms in recent years? The question seems to be one well worth pondering. Moreover, it involves comparisons and statistics which are not always infallible. It may be said with truth, however, that our people are passing through a phase of humanism, though traditionally Christian in type. None the less, such as have accepted humanism as their creed might do worse than take some of the outstanding exponents of it in Ancient Greece as their models.

But to return once more to the subject of *practical* politics, i.e. politics in the Greek sense, namely, the life of men in a community, and consider yet once again the achievements of Athens, for example, we find that almost every free citizen must, at one time or another in his life, have taken a definite and responsible part in the administration of its government. But how does this sense of responsibility compare with that of the British people, so many of whom are ignorant of, and inexperienced in, the responsibilities of office, and do not even take the trouble to vote at municipal elections?

The teaching of Civics in the United Kingdom has never been done successfully, or taken very seriously, in the majority of our schools and colleges. It is true that in some schools attended by older pupils 'mock' political elections are held; sometimes they are even admitted to the town hall to witness ceremonies connected with mayoral elections. When younger children are taken to these functions, however, the results are not always altogether so satisfactory – as, for example, when one such child described in writing the scene: 'We stood waiting for the Mayor to come in. Then an usher called out "His Worship, the Mayor" and when he came in we worshipped the Mayor and went back to school.' Nevertheless, preparation for interest in civic life should not be beyond the wit of man to devise.

It cannot be doubted that the study of Greek, as well as of its glowing literature and art, has been gradually receding in recent years in face of the engulfing tide of scientific research and achievement, even though, paradoxically enough, so many of the newly coined words used in its terminology were minted in ancient Greece. And yet there must be few modern books on politics and ethics which do not contain numerous references to Aristotle and his works. Typical of such is F. S. Marvin's estimate of the importance of both master and pupil in *The Living Past*. He writes:

> The teaching of Plato and Aristotle on moral and social questions, on education and on government, continued and will always continue of supreme interest, not only for its positive and permanent wisdom, but as representing the first reasoned answers to the largest questions in life, from the most gifted people in the world coming to them with an open mind [3].

In the matter of education, however, their views should by no means be confined to the living *past*. For, in these days, when education tends to be regarded as a thing of shreds and patches, it is indeed salutary to note that, in their view, the theory and practice of it should be built upon a solid foundation of a philosophy of life, especially in the sphere of ethics and politics. And this is the building which Aristotle, at any rate, constructs for us in his two books with those titles. Meanwhile, much as we may regret the diminution of the study of Greek in this country, we can still invoke the 'positive and *permanent* wisdom' of ancient Greece to enlighten us on some of the many perplexities which confront us in education today.

Finally, though little in this chapter has been written specifically about the literature of Ancient Greece in its relation to modern English writing, there is also much both in prose and verse styles that we can derive from it. This point was admirably expressed in a series of lectures on English Literature to a Cambridge audience by Sir Arthur Quiller-Couch some fifty years ago. Urging his hearers to embark upon the patient study of Greek and Latin authors – in the original or in translation – he gave three reasons for so doing:

> In the first place they will correct your insularity of mind; rather, will teach you to forget it. The Anglo-Saxon, it has been noted, ever left an empty space around his house: and that, no doubt, is good for a house; it is not so good for the mind. Secondly, we have a tribal habit . . . of confining our enjoyment to the written word and frowning upon the drama, the song, and

the dance . . . 'I will sing and give praise', says the scripture 'with the best member that I have' – meaning the tongue. But the old Greek was 'an all-round man' as we say. He sought to praise and give thanks with *all* his members, and to tune each to perfection. I think his way worth your considering. Lastly, and chiefly, I commend these classical authors to you because they, in the European civilization which we all inherit, conserve the norm of literature, the steady grip on the essential, the clean outline at which in verse or in prose – in epic, drama, history, or philosophical treatise – a writer should aim.

Notes

CHAPTER 1

1 *Greek Philosophy* by R. B. Appleton (English University Press).
2 *Guide to the Philosophy of Morals and Politics* by C. E. M. Joad (Victor Gollancz).
3 *Greek Genius and its meaning to us* by R. W. Livingstone (quoted by permission of the publishers, Clarendon Press, Oxford).
4 *The Age of Automation* (Reith Lecture) by Sir Leon Bagrit (Weidenfeld and Nicolson).

CHAPTER 2

1 *Greek Genius and its meaning to us* by R. W. Livingstone.

CHAPTER 3

1 *The Changing Soviet School* by George Z. F. Bereday and others (Houghton Mifflin Co., Boston).
2 *The Times Educational Supplement*, 4 September, 1964.
3 The Association for Special Education.
4 *Report of the Committee on Broadcasting*, 1960 (H.M.S.O.).

CHAPTER 4

1 *Schooling, 1963–1970* by C. H. Dobinson (Harrap).
2 The Plowden Report (H.M.S.O.).
3 Education Act, 1944 (H.M.S.O.).
3*a* See *Georg Kerschensteiner* by Diane Simons (Methuen).
4 The Association of Teachers in Technical Institutions.
5 Schools Council Examination Bulletin No. 1 (H.M.S.O.).
6 *The City State of the Greeks and Romans* by W. Warde Fowler (Macmillan).

CHAPTER 5

1 Spens Report on Secondary Education, 1938, App. 2 (H.M.S.O.).
2 Quoted in *The Times Literary Supplement*.
3 The Robbins Report, 1963 (H.M.S.O.).

4 'Technology and the Sixth Form Boy' (University of Oxford Department of Education).
5 Council for Education in World Citizenship, 25 Charles Street, London, W.1.
6 A communication from David Zeldin, a London schoolboy.
7 National Council of Social Service, 26 Bedford Square, London, W.C.1.
8 *Creating a Culture adapted to Modern Life* by Watson (Harrap).

CHAPTER 6

1 *The Harmonies of Aristoxenos* by Macran (Clarendon Press, Oxford).
2 *The New Oxford History of Music* (Oxford University Press).
3 *Musical Instruments* by K. Geiringer (Allen and Unwin).
4 *Teaching Music* by Cyril Winn (Oxford University Press).
5 *International Cyclopaedia of Music and Musicians* edited by O. Thompson (J. M. Dent).
6 *Music in Education* by George Self (Novello and Co.).

CHAPTER 7

1 Dr Milton R. Stein in *Pleasures in Learning*, Divisions magazine of General Studies at New York University.
2 *The Age of Automation* by Sir Leon Bagrit.
3. *Music Supervisors' Journal of America.*

EPILOGUE

1 Quoted from Plutarch in *Greek Genius and its Meaning to Us* by Sir R. W. Livingstone.
2 *The City State of the Greeks and Romans* by W. Warde Fowler.
3 *The Living Past* by F. S. Marvin (Clarendon Press).

Index